THIS BOOK BELONGS TO:

About this Book:

This journal is designed to help you **"PRESS FORWARD WITH A STEADFASTNESS IN CHRIST, HAVING A PERFECT BRIGHTNESS OF HOPE, AND A LOVE OF GOD AND OF ALL MEN. WHEREFORE, IF YE SHALL PRESS FORWARD, FEASTING UPON THE WORD OF CHRIST, AND ENDURE TO THE END, BEHOLD, THUS SAITH THE FATHER: YE SHALL HAVE ETERNAL LIFE."** (2 Nephi 31:20) which is the 2016 LDS mutual theme. Each day you can record significant things that happened that day as well as what you did to "Press Forward" (see page 5 for a sample page). Imagine what can happen as you spend an entire year focused on this theme!

We divided the theme up into the six principles that the scripture teaches:
* Press forward with a steadfastness in Christ
* Having a perfect brightness of hope
* Having a love of God
* Having a love of all men
* Feasting upon the word of Christ
* Enduring to the end

Each month you will focus on one part of this theme; report to yourself each day about specific things you did. You can brainstorm specific ideas of things you can do on pages 1-4, and then use those ideas as you make goals throughout the year. Imagine the things you will accomplish this year as you make this great scripture a part of your daily life!

This journal also helps you complete **ALL PERSONAL PROGRESS EXPERIENCES.** On each Sabbath day, there is a page to help you fulfill one of the experiences. The experiences that are supposed to last a number of days or weeks are built right into your daily journal so you can report to yourself every day! For example, in *Faith Experience #1* you are supposed to focus on saying your morning and evening prayers every day, so we added this right into your journal (see page 10) and kept it there for the rest of the year! Another example is on page 54 for Divine Nature Experience #2. In this experience, for two weeks you focus on a divine feminine quality you want to focus on and develop. In the journal you will report to yourself each day about what you have done to develop that important quality. Imagine the personal progress you will experience in yourself as you focus and report on these great challenges!

After putting all of the experiences on a Sabbath Day, there were a few left over. We included those experiences at the end of the journal. So remember those are there, and work on them when you have free time!

Finally, there is a **NOTE PAGE** for **CHURCH MEETINGS** and **CLASSES** (see page 6 for a sample page). You can record specific doctrines and principles you learned, tape in hand-outs, or record personal thoughts you have during your meetings and classes.

Table of Contents

WHEREFORE, YE MUST

Press forward

WITH A STEADFASTNESS IN CHRIST, HAVING A PERFECT BRIGHTNESS OF HOPE, AND A LOVE OF GOD AND OF ALL MEN. WHEREFORE, IF YE SHALL PRESS FORWARD, FEASTING UPON THE WORD OF CHRIST, AND ENDURE TO THE END, BEHOLD, THUS SAITH THE FATHER: YE SHALL HAVE ETERNAL LIFE.

2 Nephi 31:20

What do you think it means to "press forward"?

Why do you think this scripture was chosen as the 2016 mutual theme?

What important doctrines and principles you can find in this scripture?

PRESS FORWARD WITH STEADFASTNESS IN CHRIST

What do you think it means to "press forward with a steadfastness in Christ"?

STEADFAST: Fixed in direction, firm in purpose, not wavering or budging an inch.

What are some specific things you can do to "press forward with a steadfastness in Christ"?

PRESS FORWARD WITH A PERFECT BRIGHTNESS OF HOPE

What do you think it means to "press forward having a perfect brightness of hope"?

What are some specific things you can do to "press forward having a perfect brightness of hope"?

What do you think it means to "press forward having a love of God"?

What are some specific things you can do to "press forward having a love of God"?

What do you think it means to "press forward having a love of all men"?

What are some specific things you can do to "press forward having a love of all men"?

PRESS FORWARD FEASTING UPON THE WORD OF CHRIST

What do you think it means to "press forward, feasting upon the word of Christ"?

What are some specific things you can do to "press forward, feasting upon the word of Christ"?

PRESS FORWARD ENDURING TO THE END

What do you think it means to "press forward, enduring to the end"?

What are some specific things you can do to "press forward, enduring to the end"?

This journal is filled with pages to help you keep the 2016 mutual theme at the center of your life throughout the year! It will also help you fulfill all of your Personal Progress experiences!

Just fill in each day's column. It should only take you a few minutes every day, but it can have a huge impact as you report your goals and progress every day.

Each Sunday there are pages for you to take notes in sacrament meeting and your church classes. There is also a Personal Progress experience you can work on every Sunday! By the end of the year you can have all of your Personal Progress experiences completed in a meaningful way! When applicable, we included your Personal Progress experiences in the weekly columns as you track the goals that take a week or longer. This format will help make Personal Progress exciting and really meaningful!

Each month you will focus on a different portion of the 2016 mutual theme. As you make goals each day, refer to your ideas on pages 1-4.

SAMPLE PAGE

January 1-3 — PRESS FORWARD WITH A STEADFASTNESS IN CHRIST

	FRIDAY JANUARY 1ST 2016	SATURDAY JANUARY 2nd 2016	SUNDAY JANUARY 3RD 2016
SIGNIFICANT THINGS THAT HAPPENED TODAY	IT IS NEW YEAR'S DAY! We made a big breakfast and then went ice skating. mom and dad had us make new year's goals. later my friends came over and we watched a movie and made caramel popcorn.	We went to grandma and grandpa's. Grandma taught me how to make her famous rolls. We went sledding and it was really cold! When we came home dad hid in the hall closet and scared us when we went to hang up our coats. I screamed so loud! Then we made hot chocolate and put a 1,000 piece puzzle together.	I bore my testimony today during Fast and Testimony meeting. I was really scared but it felt good to share my testimony. I learned a lot about the Godhead today in Young Women's. I wrote a lot of notes. The cousins came over for dinner and we started telling funny stories and I laughed so hard I cried!
SPECIFIC THINGS I DID TODAY TO PRESS FORWARD WITH STEADFASTNESS IN CHRIST	- I made spiritual goals for the year - I spent quality time with my family - I posted a quote from general conference on instagram - we prayed together as a family and read scriptures - my friends and I chose a good and clean movie to watch	- I prayed as soon as I woke up this morning. - I read a talk from last General Conference. - I spent quality time with my family. - I read a chapter in the Book of Mormon.	**I BORE MY TESTIMONY!** - I really stayed focused during the Sacrament - I participated and took notes in class. It helped me learn a lot! - I helped my mom make cookies for the ladies she visit teaches. - I studied scriptures for 15 minutes.
GOAL(S) FOR TOMORROW TO PRESS FORWARD WITH STEADFASTNESS IN CHRIST	- Study my scriptures - Set a date to go to the temple - Be kind to my family and avoid contention - Help my mom around the house - Pray to know who I can serve	- Be on time to church - Help my mom get everyone ready for church - Think about Christ during the Sacrament **BEAR MY TESTIMONY!** - Study my scriptures - Keep the Sabbath Day holy	- Pray right when I get out of bed. - Read scriptures for 10 minutes before I go to school. - Go the extra mile in seminary - Look for someone who looks like they are lonely or need a friend - Help with Family Home Evening.

The Sabbath Day
JANUARY 3RD

❧ SACRAMENT MEETING ❧

WHAT ARE SOME SPECIFIC LESSONS YOU LEARNED & IMPRESSIONS YOU HAD DURING SACRAMENT MEETING?

"YOU ARE GOOD, BUT IT IS NOT ENOUGH JUST TO BE GOOD. YOU MUST BE GOOD FOR SOMETHING. YOU MUST CONTRIBUTE GOOD TO THE WORLD."

President Gordon B. Hinckley

- Pray each day for eyes to see what only I can do to serve others and build the Kingdom around me.
- Pay attention to those I know who make a difference.
- Pray for gifts of the Spirit that will help me to contribute good to the world.
- Story of George Albert Smith improving his signature.

❧ CLASSES ❧

WHAT IMPORTANT DOCTRINES & PRINCIPLES DID YOU LEARN IN YOUR CLASSES?

HEAVENLY FATHER

- God the Father is the Supreme Being in whom we believe and whom we worship.
- He is the ultimate Creator, Ruler, and Preserver of all things.
- He is perfect, has all power, and knows all things.
- He "has a body of flesh and bones as tangible as man's".

THE GODHEAD

The true doctrine of the Godhead was lost in the apostasy that followed the Savior's mortal ministry and the deaths of His Apostles.

Although the members of the Godhead are distinct beings with distinct roles, they are one in purpose and doctrine. They are perfectly united in bringing to pass Heavenly Father's divine plan of salvation.

JESUS CHRIST

- The Great Jehovah of the Old Testament
- The Messiah of the New Testament
- He created the earth
- Though sinless he was baptized
- He instituted the sacrament
- He gave His life to atone for the sins of all mankind
- He was resurrected
- He appeared to Joseph Smith
- He will come to earth again

THE HOLY GHOST

- The Holy Ghost is the third member of the Godhead
- He is a personage of spirit, without flesh and bones
- He is often referred to as the Holy Spirit, the Spirit of the Lord, or the Spirit
- The Holy Ghost works in harmony with Heavenly Father and Jesus Christ, fulfilling several roles to help us live righteously and receive the blessings of the gospel

> The most powerful Being in the universe is the father of your spirit. He knows you. He loves you with a perfect love.
>
> *President Dieter F. Uchtdorf*

SUNDAY NOTES

- Take this book to church with you and take notes in Sacrament Meeting and in your classes. This is a great way to keep all of the valuable doctrines and principles you are learning in one place!

- Be sure to record your personal and inspired thoughts and impressions.

- Tape your handouts right in your journal.

Personal Progress
FAITH EXPERIENCE #1
(3 WEEK EXPERIENCE)

WHAT IS FAITH?

☐ ALMA 32:17-43
☐ ETHER 12:6-22
☐ JOSEPH SMITH-HISTORY 1:11-20
☐ HEBREWS 11
☐ A GENERAL CONFERENCE TALK ABOUT FAITH (FIND ONE ON YOUR OWN)
☐ ANOTHER GENERAL CONFERENCE TALK ABOUT FAITH

The first principle of the gospel is faith in the Lord Jesus Christ. Study the references listed above and doodle, record, or draw what you learn about faith in each reference.

Faith is the substance of things hoped for, the evidence of things not seen

faith is things which are hoped for and not seen: wherefore, dispute not because ye see not, for ye receive no witness until after the trial of your faith.

FAITH IS NOT TO HAVE A PERFECT KNOWLEDGE OF THINGS; THEREFORE IF YE HAVE FAITH YE HOPE FOR THINGS WHICH ARE NOT SEEN, WHICH ARE TRUE.

FAITH DOES NOT FALL UPON US BY CHANCE OR STAY WITH US BY BIRTHRIGHT. IT IS, AS THE SCRIPTURES SAY, "SUBSTANCE ... THE EVIDENCE OF THINGS NOT SEEN." FAITH EMITS A SPIRITUAL LIGHT, AND THAT LIGHT IS DISCERNIBLE. & FAITH IN JESUS CHRIST IS A GIFT FROM HEAVEN THAT COMES AS WE CHOOSE TO BELIEVE AND AS WE SEEK IT AND HOLD ON TO IT. YOUR FAITH IS EITHER GROWING STRONGER OR BECOMING WEAKER. FAITH IS A PRINCIPLE OF POWER, IMPORTANT NOT ONLY IN THIS LIFE BUT ALSO IN OUR PROGRESSION BEYOND THE VEIL.

★ Elder Neil L. Andersen ★

TRUE FAITH IS FOCUSED IN AND ON THE LORD JESUS CHRIST AND ALWAYS LEADS TO RIGHTEOUS ACTION.

Elder David A. Bednar

Challenge:

Exercise your own faith by establishing a habit of prayer in your life. Begin by regularly saying your morning and evening prayers. After three weeks of following this pattern, discuss with a parent or leader what you have learned about faith and how daily personal prayer has strengthened your faith.

HOW DO YOU THINK THIS 3 WEEK EXPERIENCE HELP YOU PERSONALLY PROGRESS?

It will help me get into the habit of daily prayer - especially in the morning. I think it will really help center me if I pray before I go to school and take the time to think about things I really need help with.

PERSONAL PROGRESS

- On each Sunday, there is a Personal Progress experience. Some experiences take a week or more. Once you finish an experience, then you will start on another one. This journal is designed to help you get the most out of these awesome experiences!

- There were a few experiences left over at the end of the year. Those experiences are included at the end of the journal. If you have extra time on a Sunday or another night, work on those experiences.

FRIDAY **JANUARY 1ST** 2016	SATURDAY **JANUARY 2nd** 2016	SUNDAY **JANUARY 3RD** 2016
SIGNIFICANT THINGS THAT HAPPENED TODAY		
SPECIFIC THINGS I DID TODAY TO PRESS FORWARD WITH STEADFASTNESS IN CHRIST		
GOAL(S) FOR TOMORROW TO PRESS FORWARD WITH STEADFASTNESS IN CHRIST		

The Sabbath Day

➤ SACRAMENT MEETING ◄

WHAT ARE SOME SPECIFIC LESSONS YOU LEARNED & IMPRESSIONS YOU HAD DURING SACRAMENT MEETING?

➤ CLASSES ◄

WHAT IMPORTANT DOCTRINES & PRINCIPLES DID YOU LEARN IN YOUR CLASSES?

Personal Progress

FAITH EXPERIENCE #1
(3 WEEK EXPERIENCE)

WHAT IS FAITH?

☐ ALMA 32:17-43
☐ ETHER 12:6-22
☐ JOSEPH SMITH-HISTORY 1:11-20
☐ HEBREWS 11
☐ A GENERAL CONFERENCE TALK ABOUT FAITH (FIND ONE ON YOUR OWN)
☐ ANOTHER GENERAL CONFERENCE TALK ABOUT FAITH

The first principle of the gospel is faith in the Lord Jesus Christ. Study the references listed above and doodle, record, or draw what you learn about faith in each reference.

Challenge:

Exercise your own faith by establishing a habit of prayer in your life. Begin by regularly saying your morning and evening prayers. After three weeks of following this pattern, discuss with a parent or leader what you have learned about faith and how daily personal prayer has strengthened your faith.

HOW DO YOU THINK THIS 3 WEEK EXPERIENCE HELPED YOU PERSONALLY PROGRESS?

MONDAY JANUARY 4TH 2016	TUESDAY JANUARY 5TH 2016	WEDNESDAY JANUARY 6TH 2016
☐ I HAD MORNING PRAYER ☐ I HAD EVENING PRAYER	☐ I HAD MORNING PRAYER ☐ I HAD EVENING PRAYER	☐ I HAD MORNING PRAYER ☐ I HAD EVENING PRAYER

SIGNIFICANT THINGS THAT HAPPENED TODAY

SPECIFIC THINGS I DID TODAY TO PRESS FORWARD WITH STEADFASTNESS IN CHRIST

GOAL(S) FOR TOMORROW TO PRESS FORWARD WITH STEADFASTNESS IN CHRIST

THURSDAY JANUARY 7TH 2016	FRIDAY JANUARY 8TH 2016	SATURDAY JANUARY 9TH 2016
☐ I HAD MORNING PRAYER ☐ I HAD EVENING PRAYER	☐ I HAD MORNING PRAYER ☐ I HAD EVENING PRAYER	☐ I HAD MORNING PRAYER ☐ I HAD EVENING PRAYER

SIGNIFICANT THINGS THAT HAPPENED TODAY

SPECIFIC THINGS I DID TODAY TO PRESS FORWARD WITH STEADFASTNESS IN CHRIST

GOAL(S) FOR TOMORROW TO PRESS FORWARD WITH STEADFASTNESS IN CHRIST

The Sabbath Day

SACRAMENT MEETING

WHAT ARE SOME SPECIFIC LESSONS YOU LEARNED & IMPRESSIONS YOU HAD DURING SACRAMENT MEETING?

CLASSES

WHAT IMPORTANT DOCTRINES & PRINCIPLES DID YOU LEARN IN YOUR CLASSES?

Personal Progress

FAITH EXPERIENCE #1

After one week of focusing on daily personal prayer, how has this impacted your faith?

Quote: Study and mark up this quote by Elder Joseph B. Wirthlin ("Improving Our Prayers," March 2004 General Conference).

There are many reasons our prayers may lack power. Sometimes they become routine. Our prayers become hollow when we say similar words in similar ways over and over so often that the words become more of a recitation than a communication. This is what the Savior described as "vain repetitions" (see Matt. 6:7). Such prayers, He said, will not be heard.

Our beloved prophet, President Gordon B. Hinckley, has observed:

"The trouble with most of our prayers is that we give them as if we were picking up the telephone and ordering groceries—we place our order and hang up. We need to meditate, contemplate, think of what we are praying about and for and then speak to the Lord as one man speaketh to another."

Do your prayers at times sound and feel the same? Have you ever said a prayer mechanically, the words pouring forth as though cut from a machine? Do you sometimes bore yourself as you pray?

Will prayers that do not demand much of your thought merit much attention from our Heavenly Father? When you find yourself getting into a routine with your prayers, step back and think. Meditate for a while on the things for which you really are grateful. Look for them. They don't have to be grand or glorious. Sometimes we should express our gratitude for the small and simple things like the scent of the rain, the taste of your favorite food, or the sound of a loved one's voice.

Thinking of things we are grateful for is a healing balm. It helps us get outside ourselves. It changes our focus from our pains and our trials to the abundance of this beautiful world we live in.

Think of those things you truly need. Bring your goals and your hopes and your dreams to the Lord and set them before Him. Heavenly Father wants us to approach Him and ask for His divine aid. Explain to Him the trials you are facing. Set before Him your righteous desires.

Our prayers can and should be focused on the practical, everyday struggles of life. If we should pray over our crops (see Alma 34:24), then why not over other important challenges we face?

What are some specific things you could do this week to improve your daily prayers?

SUNDAY **JANUARY 10**TH 2016	MONDAY **JANUARY 11**TH 2016	TUESDAY **JANUARY 12**TH 2016
☐ I HAD MORNING PRAYER ☐ I HAD EVENING PRAYER	☐ I HAD MORNING PRAYER ☐ I HAD EVENING PRAYER	☐ I HAD MORNING PRAYER ☐ I HAD EVENING PRAYER

SIGNIFICANT THINGS THAT HAPPENED TODAY

SPECIFIC THINGS I DID TODAY TO PRESS FORWARD WITH STEADFASTNESS IN CHRIST

GOAL(S) FOR TOMORROW TO PRESS FORWARD WITH STEADFASTNESS IN CHRIST

January 13-15

PRESS FORWARD WITH A STEADFASTNESS IN CHRIST

WEDNESDAY JANUARY 13TH 2016	THURSDAY JANUARY 14TH 2016	FRIDAY JANUARY 15TH 2016
☐ I HAD MORNING PRAYER ☐ I HAD EVENING PRAYER	☐ I HAD MORNING PRAYER ☐ I HAD EVENING PRAYER	☐ I HAD MORNING PRAYER ☐ I HAD EVENING PRAYER

SIGNIFICANT THINGS THAT HAPPENED TODAY

SPECIFIC THINGS I DID TODAY TO PRESS FORWARD WITH STEADFASTNESS IN CHRIST

GOAL(S) FOR TOMORROW TO PRESS FORWARD WITH STEADFASTNESS IN CHRIST

SATURDAY **JANUARY 16**TH 2016	SUNDAY **JANUARY 17**TH 2016	MONDAY **JANUARY 18**TH 2016
☐ I HAD MORNING PRAYER ☐ I HAD EVENING PRAYER	☐ I HAD MORNING PRAYER ☐ I HAD EVENING PRAYER	☐ I HAD MORNING PRAYER ☐ I HAD EVENING PRAYER

SIGNIFICANT THINGS THAT HAPPENED TODAY

SPECIFIC THINGS I DID TODAY TO PRESS FORWARD WITH STEADFASTNESS IN CHRIST

GOAL(S) FOR TOMORROW TO PRESS FORWARD WITH STEADFASTNESS IN CHRIST

The Sabbath Day

≫ SACRAMENT MEETING ≪

WHAT ARE SOME SPECIFIC LESSONS YOU LEARNED & IMPRESSIONS YOU HAD DURING SACRAMENT MEETING?

≫ CLASSES ≪

WHAT IMPORTANT DOCTRINES & PRINCIPLES DID YOU LEARN IN YOUR CLASSES?

After two weeks of focusing on daily personal prayer, how has this impacted your faith?

Quote: Study and mark up this quote by Elder Joseph B. Wirthlin ("Improving Our Prayers," March 2004 General Conference).

Another reason many prayers have little power is that we lack faith. We approach our Heavenly Father like a child who asks something of his or her parents, knowing they will refuse. Without faith, our prayers are merely words. With faith, our prayers connect with the powers of heaven and can bring upon us increased understanding, hope, and power. If by faith the worlds were created, then by faith we can create and receive the righteous desires of our heart....

Faith without works is dead. Sometimes we expect Heavenly Father to answer our prayers when all we have done is utter a prayer. The doors of heaven will ever be closed to those who hold out their hands, waiting for blessings to drop from heaven upon them.

The powers of faith are activated by action. We must do our part. We must prepare. We must do all that is in our power, and we will be blessed in our efforts.

Prayer is a private matter between you and Heavenly Father. Both He and you know when you have done what you can. Do not give a thought as to whether or not your best compares with others. In the eyes of Heavenly Father, that doesn't matter.

Another reason our prayers have little power is that we fail to succor those in need around us. The Book of Mormon teaches, "If ye turn away the needy, and the naked, and visit not the sick and afflicted, and impart of your substance, if ye have, to those who stand in need—I say unto you, if ye do not any of these things, behold, your prayer is vain, and availeth you nothing" (Alma 34:28).

Our willingness to aid those in distress around us has ever been the benchmark of the disciples of Christ. Indeed, the Savior taught that our very salvation depends upon the level of our compassion for others (see Matt. 25:31–46). If we turn our backs upon the poor and the distressed, can we, in turn, suppose that our Heavenly Father will be merciful to us? As we are to those in need, so our Heavenly Father will be to us in our time of need.

What are some specific things you could do this week to improve your daily prayers?

January 19-21 ❧ PRESS FORWARD WITH A STEADFASTNESS IN CHRIST

TUESDAY JANUARY 19TH 2016	WEDNESDAY JANUARY 20TH 2016	THURSDAY JANUARY 21ST 2016
☐ I HAD MORNING PRAYER ☐ I HAD EVENING PRAYER	☐ I HAD MORNING PRAYER ☐ I HAD EVENING PRAYER	☐ I HAD MORNING PRAYER ☐ I HAD EVENING PRAYER

SIGNIFICANT THINGS THAT HAPPENED TODAY

SPECIFIC THINGS I DID TODAY TO PRESS FORWARD WITH STEADFASTNESS IN CHRIST

GOAL(S) FOR TOMORROW TO PRESS FORWARD WITH STEADFASTNESS IN CHRIST

FRIDAY **JANUARY 22ND** 2016	SATURDAY **JANUARY 23RD** 2016	SUNDAY **JANUARY 24TH** 2016
☐ I HAD MORNING PRAYER ☐ I HAD EVENING PRAYER	☐ I HAD MORNING PRAYER ☐ I HAD EVENING PRAYER	☐ I HAD MORNING PRAYER ☐ I HAD EVENING PRAYER

SIGNIFICANT THINGS THAT HAPPENED TODAY

SPECIFIC THINGS I DID TODAY TO PRESS FORWARD WITH STEADFASTNESS IN CHRIST

GOAL(S) FOR TOMORROW TO PRESS FORWARD WITH STEADFASTNESS IN CHRIST

The Sabbath Day

SACRAMENT MEETING

WHAT ARE SOME SPECIFIC LESSONS YOU LEARNED & IMPRESSIONS YOU HAD DURING SACRAMENT MEETING?

CLASSES

WHAT IMPORTANT DOCTRINES & PRINCIPLES DID YOU LEARN IN YOUR CLASSES?

FAITH EXPERIENCE #1

After three weeks of focusing on daily personal prayer, how has this impacted your faith?

What else have you learned from this challenge?

How has this experience helped you personally progress?

Now that the three week challenge is over, what personal commitments would you like to make to yourself to be sure that you continue to do the things you learned from this experience?

MONDAY **JANUARY 25TH** 2016	TUESDAY **JANUARY 26TH** 2016	WEDNESDAY **JANUARY 27TH** 2016
☐ I HAD MORNING PRAYER ☐ I HAD EVENING PRAYER	☐ I HAD MORNING PRAYER ☐ I HAD EVENING PRAYER	☐ I HAD MORNING PRAYER ☐ I HAD EVENING PRAYER

SIGNIFICANT THINGS THAT HAPPENED TODAY

SPECIFIC THINGS I DID TODAY TO PRESS FORWARD WITH STEADFASTNESS IN CHRIST

GOAL(S) FOR TOMORROW TO PRESS FORWARD WITH STEADFASTNESS IN CHRIST

THURSDAY **JANUARY 28TH** 2016	FRIDAY **JANUARY 29TH** 2016	SATURDAY **JANUARY 30TH** 2016
☐ I HAD MORNING PRAYER ☐ I HAD EVENING PRAYER	☐ I HAD MORNING PRAYER ☐ I HAD EVENING PRAYER	☐ I HAD MORNING PRAYER ☐ I HAD EVENING PRAYER
		SIGNIFICANT THINGS THAT HAPPENED TODAY
		SPECIFIC THINGS I DID TODAY TO PRESS FORWARD WITH STEADFASTNESS IN CHRIST
		GOAL(S) FOR TOMORROW TO PRESS FORWARD WITH STEADFASTNESS IN CHRIST

The Sabbath Day

SACRAMENT MEETING

WHAT ARE SOME SPECIFIC LESSONS YOU LEARNED & IMPRESSIONS YOU HAD DURING SACRAMENT MEETING?

CLASSES

WHAT IMPORTANT DOCTRINES & PRINCIPLES DID YOU LEARN IN YOUR CLASSES?

WOMANHOOD & FAITH

What do the mothers of the stripling warriors teach you about faith in Alma 56:45-48 and 57:21?

Study "The Family: A Proclamation to the World". What do you learn about a mother's role?

Ask your mother, grandmother, or leader this question: WHAT QUALITIES DOES A WOMAN NEED IN ORDER TO TEACH CHILDREN TO HAVE FAITH AND BASE THEIR DECISIONS ON GOSPEL TRUTHS? Record what you learn.

What can you do to prepare to be a faithful woman, wife, and mother?

PRESS FORWARD WITH A
PERFECT BRIGHTNESS OF HOPE

SUNDAY **JANUARY 31ST** 2016	MONDAY **FEBRUARY 1ST** 2016	TUESDAY **FEBRUARY 2ND** 2016
☐ I HAD MORNING PRAYER ☐ I HAD EVENING PRAYER	☐ I HAD MORNING PRAYER ☐ I HAD EVENING PRAYER	☐ I HAD MORNING PRAYER ☐ I HAD EVENING PRAYER

SIGNIFICANT THINGS THAT HAPPENED TODAY

SPECIFIC THINGS I DID TODAY TO PRESS FORWARD WITH A PERFECT BRIGHTNESS OF HOPE

GOAL(S) FOR TOMORROW TO PRESS FORWARD WITH A PERFECT BRIGHTNESS OF HOPE

WEDNESDAY **FEBRUARY 3RD** 2016	THURSDAY **FEBRUARY 4TH** 2016	FRIDAY **FEBRUARY 5TH** 2016
☐ I HAD MORNING PRAYER ☐ I HAD EVENING PRAYER	☐ I HAD MORNING PRAYER ☐ I HAD EVENING PRAYER	☐ I HAD MORNING PRAYER ☐ I HAD EVENING PRAYER

SIGNIFICANT THINGS THAT HAPPENED TODAY

SPECIFIC THINGS I DID TODAY TO PRESS FORWARD WITH A PERFECT BRIGHTNESS OF HOPE

GOAL(S) FOR TOMORROW TO PRESS FORWARD WITH A PERFECT BRIGHTNESS OF HOPE

SATURDAY **FEBRUARY 6**TH 2016	SUNDAY **FEBRUARY 7**TH 2016	MONDAY **FEBRUARY 8**TH 2016
☐ I HAD MORNING PRAYER ☐ I HAD EVENING PRAYER	☐ I HAD MORNING PRAYER ☐ I HAD EVENING PRAYER	☐ I HAD MORNING PRAYER ☐ I HAD EVENING PRAYER

SIGNIFICANT THINGS THAT HAPPENED TODAY

SPECIFIC THINGS I DID TODAY TO PRESS FORWARD WITH A PERFECT BRIGHTNESS OF HOPE

GOAL(S) FOR TOMORROW TO PRESS FORWARD WITH A PERFECT BRIGHTNESS OF HOPE

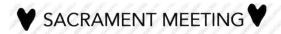

The Sabbath Day

FEBRUARY 7TH

♥ SACRAMENT MEETING ♥ WHAT ARE SOME SPECIFIC LESSONS YOU LEARNED & IMPRESSIONS YOU HAD DURING SACRAMENT MEETING?

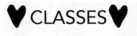 ♥ CLASSES ♥ WHAT IMPORTANT DOCTRINES & PRINCIPLES DID YOU LEARN IN YOUR CLASSES?

Personal Progress

FAITH EXPERIENCE #3

Study "Faith" in *True to the Faith*. Record significant things you learn in the space below.

Study "Faith" in the *Bible Dictionary*. Record significant things you learn in the space below.

Choose one of the following principles. Circle it.

PRAYER   FASTING   TITHING   REPENTANCE   KEEPING THE SABBATH DAY HOLY

How has faith helped you live the principle you circled above?

Give a Family Home Evening lesson about the principle you circled on the last page and how faith is required to live that principle . Use this page to plan your lesson.

TOPIC:

HYMN/SONG:

PRAYER:

LESSON OUTLINE:

february 9-11

PRESS FORWARD WITH A
PERFECT BRIGHTNESS OF HOPE

TUESDAY FEBRUARY 9TH 2016	WEDNESDAY FEBRUARY 10TH 2016	THURSDAY FEBRUARY 11TH 2016
☐ I HAD MORNING PRAYER ☐ I HAD EVENING PRAYER	☐ I HAD MORNING PRAYER ☐ I HAD EVENING PRAYER	☐ I HAD MORNING PRAYER ☐ I HAD EVENING PRAYER

SIGNIFICANT THINGS THAT HAPPENED TODAY

SPECIFIC THINGS I DID TODAY TO PRESS FORWARD WITH A PERFECT BRIGHTNESS OF HOPE

GOAL(S) FOR TOMORROW TO PRESS FORWARD WITH A PERFECT BRIGHTNESS OF HOPE

PRESS FORWARD WITH A
PERFECT BRIGHTNESS OF HOPE

february 12-14

FRIDAY **FEBRUARY 12**TH 2016	SATURDAY **FEBRUARY 13**TH 2016	SUNDAY **FEBRUARY 14**TH 2016
☐ I HAD MORNING PRAYER ☐ I HAD EVENING PRAYER	☐ I HAD MORNING PRAYER ☐ I HAD EVENING PRAYER	☐ I HAD MORNING PRAYER ☐ I HAD EVENING PRAYER

SIGNIFICANT THINGS THAT HAPPENED TODAY

SPECIFIC THINGS I DID TODAY TO PRESS FORWARD WITH A PERFECT BRIGHTNESS OF HOPE

GOAL(S) FOR TOMORROW TO PRESS FORWARD WITH A PERFECT BRIGHTNESS OF HOPE

The Sabbath Day

FEBRUARY 14TH

♥ SACRAMENT MEETING ♥ WHAT ARE SOME SPECIFIC LESSONS YOU LEARNED & IMPRESSIONS YOU HAD DURING SACRAMENT MEETING?

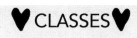 ♥ CLASSES ♥ WHAT IMPORTANT DOCTRINES & PRINCIPLES DID YOU LEARN IN YOUR CLASSES?

YOU MUST FULFILL 3 ADDITIONAL "FAITH" EXPERIENCES. USE THIS PAGE TO COMPLETE ONE OF THE ADDITIONAL EXPERIENCES FOUND IN YOUR PERSONAL PROGRESS BOOK.

Personal Progress

FIRST ADDITIONAL FAITH EXPERIENCE

MONDAY FEBRUARY 15TH 2016	TUESDAY FEBRUARY 16TH 2016	WEDNESDAY FEBRUARY 17TH 2016
☐ I HAD MORNING PRAYER ☐ I HAD EVENING PRAYER	☐ I HAD MORNING PRAYER ☐ I HAD EVENING PRAYER	☐ I HAD MORNING PRAYER ☐ I HAD EVENING PRAYER

SIGNIFICANT THINGS THAT HAPPENED TODAY

SPECIFIC THINGS I DID TODAY TO PRESS FORWARD WITH A PERFECT BRIGHTNESS OF HOPE

GOAL(S) FOR TOMORROW TO PRESS FORWARD WITH A PERFECT BRIGHTNESS OF HOPE

THURSDAY FEBRUARY 18TH 2016	FRIDAY FEBRUARY 19TH 2016	SATURDAY FEBRUARY 20TH 2016
☐ I HAD MORNING PRAYER ☐ I HAD EVENING PRAYER	☐ I HAD MORNING PRAYER ☐ I HAD EVENING PRAYER	☐ I HAD MORNING PRAYER ☐ I HAD EVENING PRAYER

SIGNIFICANT THINGS THAT HAPPENED TODAY

SPECIFIC THINGS I DID TODAY TO PRESS FORWARD WITH A PERFECT BRIGHTNESS OF HOPE

GOAL(S) FOR TOMORROW TO PRESS FORWARD WITH A PERFECT BRIGHTNESS OF HOPE

The Sabbath Day

FEBRUARY 21ST

♥ SACRAMENT MEETING ♥ WHAT ARE SOME SPECIFIC LESSONS YOU LEARNED & IMPRESSIONS YOU HAD DURING SACRAMENT MEETING?

 ♥ CLASSES ♥ WHAT IMPORTANT DOCTRINES & PRINCIPLES DID YOU LEARN IN YOUR CLASSES?

YOU MUST FULFILL 3 ADDITIONAL "FAITH" EXPERIENCES. USE THIS PAGE
TO COMPLETE ONE OF THE ADDITIONAL EXPERIENCES FOUND IN YOUR
PERSONAL PROGRESS BOOK.

Personal Progress
SECOND ADDITIONAL FAITH EXPERIENCE

SUNDAY **FEBRUARY 21**ST 2016	MONDAY **FEBRUARY 22**ND 2016	TUESDAY **FEBRUARY 23**RD 2016
☐ I HAD MORNING PRAYER ☐ I HAD EVENING PRAYER	☐ I HAD MORNING PRAYER ☐ I HAD EVENING PRAYER	☐ I HAD MORNING PRAYER ☐ I HAD EVENING PRAYER

SIGNIFICANT THINGS THAT HAPPENED TODAY

SPECIFIC THINGS I DID TODAY TO PRESS FORWARD WITH A PERFECT BRIGHTNESS OF HOPE

GOAL(S) FOR TOMORROW TO PRESS FORWARD WITH A PERFECT BRIGHTNESS OF HOPE

WEDNESDAY **FEBRUARY 24**TH 2016	THURSDAY **FEBRUARY 25**TH 2016	FRIDAY **FEBRUARY 26**TH 2016
☐ I HAD MORNING PRAYER ☐ I HAD EVENING PRAYER	☐ I HAD MORNING PRAYER ☐ I HAD EVENING PRAYER	☐ I HAD MORNING PRAYER ☐ I HAD EVENING PRAYER

SIGNIFICANT THINGS THAT HAPPENED TODAY

SPECIFIC THINGS I DID TODAY TO PRESS FORWARD WITH A PERFECT BRIGHTNESS OF HOPE

GOAL(S) FOR TOMORROW TO PRESS FORWARD WITH A PERFECT BRIGHTNESS OF HOPE

february 27-29 ♥♥ PRESS FORWARD WITH A
PERFECT BRIGHTNESS OF HOPE

SATURDAY FEBRUARY 27TH 2016	SUNDAY FEBRUARY 28TH 2016	MONDAY FEBRUARY 29TH 2016
☐ I HAD MORNING PRAYER ☐ I HAD EVENING PRAYER	☐ I HAD MORNING PRAYER ☐ I HAD EVENING PRAYER	☐ I HAD MORNING PRAYER ☐ I HAD EVENING PRAYER

SIGNIFICANT THINGS THAT HAPPENED TODAY

SPECIFIC THINGS I DID TODAY TO PRESS FORWARD WITH A PERFECT BRIGHTNESS OF HOPE

GOAL(S) FOR TOMORROW TO PRESS FORWARD WITH A PERFECT BRIGHTNESS OF HOPE

 SACRAMENT MEETING

WHAT ARE SOME SPECIFIC LESSONS YOU LEARNED & IMPRESSIONS YOU HAD DURING SACRAMENT MEETING?

 CLASSES

WHAT IMPORTANT DOCTRINES & PRINCIPLES DID YOU LEARN IN YOUR CLASSES?

Personal Progress

THIRD ADDITIONAL FAITH EXPERIENCE

YOU MUST FULFILL 3 ADDITIONAL "FAITH" EXPERIENCES. USE THIS PAGE TO COMPLETE ONE OF THE ADDITIONAL EXPERIENCES FOUND IN YOUR PERSONAL PROGRESS BOOK.

TUESDAY **MARCH 1ST** 2016	WEDNESDAY **MARCH 2ND** 2016	THURSDAY **MARCH 3RD** 2016
☐ I HAD MORNING PRAYER ☐ I HAD EVENING PRAYER	☐ I HAD MORNING PRAYER ☐ I HAD EVENING PRAYER	☐ I HAD MORNING PRAYER ☐ I HAD EVENING PRAYER

SIGNIFICANT THINGS THAT HAPPENED TODAY

SPECIFIC THINGS I DID TODAY TO PRESS FORWARD WITH A LOVE OF GOD

GOAL(S) FOR TOMORROW TO PRESS FORWARD WITH A LOVE OF GOD

March 4-6

PRESS FORWARD WITH A LOVE OF GOD

FRIDAY MARCH 4TH 2016	SATURDAY MARCH 5TH 2016	SUNDAY MARCH 6TH 2016
☐ I HAD MORNING PRAYER ☐ I HAD EVENING PRAYER	☐ I HAD MORNING PRAYER ☐ I HAD EVENING PRAYER	☐ I HAD MORNING PRAYER ☐ I HAD EVENING PRAYER

SIGNIFICANT THINGS THAT HAPPENED TODAY

SPECIFIC THINGS I DID TODAY TO PRESS FORWARD WITH A LOVE OF GOD

GOAL(S) FOR TOMORROW TO PRESS FORWARD WITH A LOVE OF GOD

The Sabbath Day

MARCH 6TH

SACRAMENT MEETING

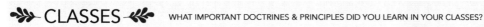 WHAT ARE SOME SPECIFIC LESSONS YOU LEARNED & IMPRESSIONS YOU HAD DURING SACRAMENT MEETING?

CLASSES

WHAT IMPORTANT DOCTRINES & PRINCIPLES DID YOU LEARN IN YOUR CLASSES?

DIVINE QUALITIES OF DAUGHTERS OF GOD

What divine qualities do daughters of God have?   Study the references below and doodle, record, or draw what you learn from each reference.

| THE FAMILY: A PROCLAMATION TO THE WORLD | 2 PETER 1 |

| ALMA 7:23-24 | DOCTRINE & COVENANTS 121:45 |

Pick five of the qualities you listed above. Record them below along with ideas of how you can develop those qualities within yourself.

QUALITY	WHAT YOU CAN DO TO DEVELOP THAT QUALITY

March 7-9

MONDAY **MARCH 7**TH 2016	TUESDAY **MARCH 8**TH 2016	WEDNESDAY **MARCH 9**TH 2016
☐ I HAD MORNING PRAYER ☐ I HAD EVENING PRAYER	☐ I HAD MORNING PRAYER ☐ I HAD EVENING PRAYER	☐ I HAD MORNING PRAYER ☐ I HAD EVENING PRAYER

SIGNIFICANT THINGS THAT HAPPENED TODAY

SPECIFIC THINGS I DID TODAY TO PRESS FORWARD WITH A LOVE OF GOD

GOAL(S) FOR TOMORROW TO PRESS FORWARD WITH A LOVE OF GOD

THURSDAY **MARCH 10**TH 2016	FRIDAY **MARCH 11**TH 2016	SATURDAY **MARCH 12**TH 2016
☐ I HAD MORNING PRAYER ☐ I HAD EVENING PRAYER	☐ I HAD MORNING PRAYER ☐ I HAD EVENING PRAYER	☐ I HAD MORNING PRAYER ☐ I HAD EVENING PRAYER

SIGNIFICANT THINGS THAT HAPPENED TODAY

SPECIFIC THINGS I DID TODAY TO PRESS FORWARD WITH A LOVE OF GOD

GOAL(S) FOR TOMORROW TO PRESS FORWARD WITH A LOVE OF GOD

SACRAMENT MEETING

WHAT ARE SOME SPECIFIC LESSONS YOU LEARNED & IMPRESSIONS YOU HAD DURING SACRAMENT MEETING?

CLASSES

WHAT IMPORTANT DOCTRINES & PRINCIPLES DID YOU LEARN IN YOUR CLASSES?

Personal Progress

DIVINE NATURE EXPERIENCE #2

DIVINE FEMININE QUALITIES

-THE FAMILY: A PROCLAMATION TO THE WORLD
-PROVERBS 31:10-31
-TWO GENERAL CONFERENCE TALKS ON WOMANHOOD

As a young woman you are blessed with divine feminine qualities. Increase your understanding of those divine qualities by studying the references to the above right. Record the divine feminine qualities you find in those references.

Talk to your mother or a mother you admire. Ask her what she thinks are important attributes for being a mother. List the attributes below.

Choose one of those attributes that you would like to develop and write it in the banner. Over the next two weeks strive to develop that quality. In the box below record specific things you can do to develop that quality.

SUNDAY **MARCH 13**TH 2016	MONDAY **MARCH 14**TH 2016	TUESDAY **MARCH 15**TH 2016	
☐ I HAD MORNING PRAYER ☐ I HAD EVENING PRAYER	☐ I HAD MORNING PRAYER ☐ I HAD EVENING PRAYER	☐ I HAD MORNING PRAYER ☐ I HAD EVENING PRAYER	
			SIGNIFICANT THINGS THAT HAPPENED TODAY
			SPECIFIC THINGS I DID TODAY TO PRESS FORWARD WITH A LOVE OF GOD
			GOAL(S) FOR TOMORROW TO PRESS FORWARD WITH A LOVE OF GOD
			WHAT YOU DID TO DEVELOP THE DIVINE QUALITY YOU CHOSE ON PAGE 53

WEDNESDAY **MARCH 16**TH 2016	THURSDAY **MARCH 17**TH 2016	FRIDAY **MARCH 18**TH 2016
☐ I HAD MORNING PRAYER ☐ I HAD EVENING PRAYER	☐ I HAD MORNING PRAYER ☐ I HAD EVENING PRAYER	☐ I HAD MORNING PRAYER ☐ I HAD EVENING PRAYER

SIGNIFICANT THINGS THAT HAPPENED TODAY

SPECIFIC THINGS I DID TODAY TO PRESS FORWARD WITH A LOVE OF GOD

GOAL(S) FOR TOMORROW TO PRESS FORWARD WITH A LOVE OF GOD

WHAT YOU DID TO DEVELOP THE DIVINE QUALITY YOU CHOSE ON PAGE 53

March 19-21

SATURDAY **MARCH 19**TH 2016	SUNDAY **MARCH 20**TH 2016	MONDAY **MARCH 21**ST 2016
☐ I HAD MORNING PRAYER ☐ I HAD EVENING PRAYER	☐ I HAD MORNING PRAYER ☐ I HAD EVENING PRAYER	☐ I HAD MORNING PRAYER ☐ I HAD EVENING PRAYER

SIGNIFICANT THINGS THAT HAPPENED TODAY

SPECIFIC THINGS I DID TODAY TO PRESS FORWARD WITH A LOVE OF GOD

GOAL(S) FOR TOMORROW TO PRESS FORWARD WITH A LOVE OF GOD

WHAT YOU DID TO DEVELOP THE DIVINE QUALITY YOU CHOSE ON PAGE 53

The Sabbath Day

MARCH 20TH

SACRAMENT MEETING

WHAT ARE SOME SPECIFIC LESSONS YOU LEARNED & IMPRESSIONS YOU HAD DURING SACRAMENT MEETING?

CLASSES

WHAT IMPORTANT DOCTRINES & PRINCIPLES DID YOU LEARN IN YOUR CLASSES?

DIVINE FEMININE QUALITIES

What have you learned this week as you have worked on developing the divine feminine quality you chose?

What are you going to do this week to continue to develop that quality?

March 22-24

	TUESDAY MARCH 22nd 2016	WEDNESDAY MARCH 23RD 2016	THURSDAY MARCH 24TH 2016
	☐ I HAD MORNING PRAYER ☐ I HAD EVENING PRAYER	☐ I HAD MORNING PRAYER ☐ I HAD EVENING PRAYER	☐ I HAD MORNING PRAYER ☐ I HAD EVENING PRAYER
SIGNIFICANT THINGS THAT HAPPENED TODAY			
SPECIFIC THINGS I DID TODAY TO PRESS FORWARD WITH A LOVE OF GOD			
GOAL(S) FOR TOMORROW TO PRESS FORWARD WITH A LOVE OF GOD			
WHAT YOU DID TO DEVELOP THE DIVINE QUALITY YOU CHOSE ON PAGE 53			

March 25-27

FRIDAY MARCH 25TH 2016	SATURDAY MARCH 26TH 2016	SUNDAY MARCH 27TH 2016
☐ I HAD MORNING PRAYER ☐ I HAD EVENING PRAYER	☐ I HAD MORNING PRAYER ☐ I HAD EVENING PRAYER	☐ I HAD MORNING PRAYER ☐ I HAD EVENING PRAYER

SIGNIFICANT THINGS THAT HAPPENED TODAY

SPECIFIC THINGS I DID TODAY TO PRESS FORWARD WITH A LOVE OF GOD

GOAL(S) FOR TOMORROW TO PRESS FORWARD WITH A LOVE OF GOD

WHAT YOU DID TO DEVELOP THE DIVINE QUALITY YOU CHOSE ON PAGE 53

The Sabbath Day

MARCH 27TH

SACRAMENT MEETING
WHAT ARE SOME SPECIFIC LESSONS YOU LEARNED & IMPRESSIONS YOU HAD DURING SACRAMENT MEETING?

CLASSES
WHAT IMPORTANT DOCTRINES & PRINCIPLES DID YOU LEARN IN YOUR CLASSES?

LOVE THROUGH ACTIONS

Make your home life better. For two weeks, make a special effort to strengthen your relationship with a family member by showing love through your actions. Refrain from judging, criticizing, or speaking unkindly. Watch for positive qualities in that family member.

You could:

- ❧ WRITE NOTES OF ENCOURAGEMENT
- ❧ PRAY FOR FAMILY MEMBERS
- ❧ FIND WAYS TO BE HELPFUL
- ❧ VERBALLY EXPRESS YOUR LOVE

Make a list of specific things you can do over the next two weeks.

What divine characteristics do you think you may develop as you fulfill this challenge?

MONDAY MARCH 28TH 2016	TUESDAY MARCH 29TH 2016	WEDNESDAY MARCH 30TH 2016
☐ I HAD MORNING PRAYER ☐ I HAD EVENING PRAYER	☐ I HAD MORNING PRAYER ☐ I HAD EVENING PRAYER	☐ I HAD MORNING PRAYER ☐ I HAD EVENING PRAYER

SIGNIFICANT THINGS THAT HAPPENED TODAY

SPECIFIC THINGS I DID TODAY TO PRESS FORWARD WITH A LOVE OF GOD

GOAL(S) FOR TOMORROW TO PRESS FORWARD WITH A LOVE OF GOD

WHAT YOU DID TO STRENGTHEN YOUR FAMILY RELATIONSHIPS

PRESS FORWARD WITH A LOVE OF ALL MEN

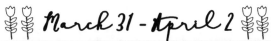 *March 31 - April 2*

THURSDAY **MARCH 31**ST 2016	FRIDAY **APRIL 1**ST 2016	SATURDAY **APRIL 2**ND 2016
☐ I HAD MORNING PRAYER ☐ I HAD EVENING PRAYER	☐ I HAD MORNING PRAYER ☐ I HAD EVENING PRAYER	☐ I HAD MORNING PRAYER ☐ I HAD EVENING PRAYER
		SIGNIFICANT THINGS THAT HAPPENED TODAY
		SPECIFIC THINGS I DID TODAY TO PRESS FORWARD WITH A LOVE OF ALL MEN
		GOAL(S) FOR TOMORROW TO PRESS FORWARD WITH A LOVE OF ALL MEN
		WHAT YOU DID TO STRENGTHEN YOUR FAMILY RELATIONSHIPS

General Conference

APRIL 3RD

LESSONS LEARNED WHAT LESSONS STOOD OUT TO YOU MOST DURING GENERAL CONFERENCE?

PERSONAL GOALS WHAT PERSONAL GOALS WOULD YOU LIKE TO MAKE BECAUSE OF WHAT YOU LEARNED?

What have you learned this week as you have made a special effort to strengthen your relationship with your family?

What special qualities have you noticed in your family members this past week?

What divine characteristics have you discovered and exercised as you have worked on this challenge?

What are some specific things you will do this next week as you continue to work on this challenge?

 April 3-5

PRESS FORWARD WITH A
LOVE OF ALL MEN

	SUNDAY **APRIL 3RD** 2016	MONDAY **APRIL 4TH** 2016	TUESDAY **APRIL 5TH** 2016
	☐ I HAD MORNING PRAYER ☐ I HAD EVENING PRAYER	☐ I HAD MORNING PRAYER ☐ I HAD EVENING PRAYER	☐ I HAD MORNING PRAYER ☐ I HAD EVENING PRAYER
SIGNIFICANT THINGS THAT HAPPENED TODAY			
SPECIFIC THINGS I DID TODAY TO PRESS FORWARD WITH A LOVE OF ALL MEN			
GOAL(S) FOR TOMORROW TO PRESS FORWARD WITH A LOVE OF ALL MEN			
WHAT YOU DID TO STRENGTHEN YOUR FAMILY RELATIONSHIPS			

PRESS FORWARD WITH A LOVE OF ALL MEN

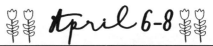 *april 6-8*

WEDNESDAY **APRIL 6**TH 2016	THURSDAY **APRIL 7**TH 2016	FRIDAY **APRIL 8**TH 2016	
☐ I HAD MORNING PRAYER ☐ I HAD EVENING PRAYER	☐ I HAD MORNING PRAYER ☐ I HAD EVENING PRAYER	☐ I HAD MORNING PRAYER ☐ I HAD EVENING PRAYER	
			SIGNIFICANT THINGS THAT HAPPENED TODAY
			SPECIFIC THINGS I DID TODAY TO PRESS FORWARD WITH A LOVE OF ALL MEN
			GOAL(S) FOR TOMORROW TO PRESS FORWARD WITH A LOVE OF ALL MEN
			WHAT YOU DID TO STRENGTHEN YOUR FAMILY RELATIONSHIPS

April 9-11

SATURDAY **APRIL 9**TH 2016	SUNDAY **APRIL 10**TH 2016	MONDAY **APRIL 11**TH 2016
☐ I HAD MORNING PRAYER ☐ I HAD EVENING PRAYER	☐ I HAD MORNING PRAYER ☐ I HAD EVENING PRAYER	☐ I HAD MORNING PRAYER ☐ I HAD EVENING PRAYER

SIGNIFICANT THINGS THAT HAPPENED TODAY

SPECIFIC THINGS I DID TODAY TO PRESS FORWARD WITH A LOVE OF ALL MEN

GOAL(S) FOR TOMORROW TO PRESS FORWARD WITH A LOVE OF ALL MEN

WHAT YOU DID TO STRENGTHEN YOUR FAMILY RELATIONSHIPS

SACRAMENT MEETING

WHAT ARE SOME SPECIFIC LESSONS YOU LEARNED &
IMPRESSIONS YOU HAD DURING SACRAMENT MEETING?

 ## CLASSES

WHAT IMPORTANT DOCTRINES & PRINCIPLES DID YOU LEARN IN YOUR CLASSES?

YOU MUST FULFILL 3 ADDITIONAL "DIVINE NATURE" EXPERIENCES. USE THIS PAGE TO COMPLETE ONE OF THE ADDITIONAL EXPERIENCES FOUND IN YOUR PERSONAL PROGRESS BOOK.

PRESS FORWARD WITH A LOVE OF ALL MEN

 April 12-14

TUESDAY **APRIL 12TH** 2016	WEDNESDAY **APRIL 13TH** 2016	THURSDAY **APRIL 14TH** 2016
☐ I HAD MORNING PRAYER ☐ I HAD EVENING PRAYER	☐ I HAD MORNING PRAYER ☐ I HAD EVENING PRAYER	☐ I HAD MORNING PRAYER ☐ I HAD EVENING PRAYER

SIGNIFICANT THINGS THAT HAPPENED TODAY

SPECIFIC THINGS I DID TODAY TO PRESS FORWARD WITH A LOVE OF ALL MEN

GOAL(S) FOR TOMORROW TO PRESS FORWARD WITH A LOVE OF ALL MEN

 april 15-17

PRESS FORWARD WITH A
LOVE OF ALL MEN

FRIDAY **APRIL 15**TH 2016	SATURDAY **APRIL 16**TH 2016	SUNDAY **APRIL 17**TH 2016
☐ I HAD MORNING PRAYER ☐ I HAD EVENING PRAYER	☐ I HAD MORNING PRAYER ☐ I HAD EVENING PRAYER	☐ I HAD MORNING PRAYER ☐ I HAD EVENING PRAYER

SIGNIFICANT THINGS THAT HAPPENED TODAY

SPECIFIC THINGS I DID TODAY TO PRESS FORWARD WITH A LOVE OF ALL MEN

GOAL(S) FOR TOMORROW TO PRESS FORWARD WITH A LOVE OF ALL MEN

SACRAMENT MEETING

WHAT ARE SOME SPECIFIC LESSONS YOU LEARNED & IMPRESSIONS YOU HAD DURING SACRAMENT MEETING?

CLASSES

WHAT IMPORTANT DOCTRINES & PRINCIPLES DID YOU LEARN IN YOUR CLASSES?

Personal Progress

SECOND ADDITIONAL DIVINE NATURE EXPERIENCE

YOU MUST FULFILL 3 ADDITIONAL "DIVINE NATURE" EXPERIENCES. USE THIS PAGE TO COMPLETE ONE OF THE ADDITIONAL EXPERIENCES FOUND IN YOUR PERSONAL PROGRESS BOOK.

MONDAY **APRIL 18**TH 2016	TUESDAY **APRIL 19**TH 2016	WEDNESDAY **APRIL 20**TH 2016
☐ I HAD MORNING PRAYER ☐ I HAD EVENING PRAYER	☐ I HAD MORNING PRAYER ☐ I HAD EVENING PRAYER	☐ I HAD MORNING PRAYER ☐ I HAD EVENING PRAYER

SIGNIFICANT THINGS THAT HAPPENED TODAY

SPECIFIC THINGS I DID TODAY TO PRESS FORWARD WITH A LOVE OF ALL MEN

GOAL(S) FOR TOMORROW TO PRESS FORWARD WITH A LOVE OF ALL MEN

 April 21-23

PRESS FORWARD WITH A
LOVE OF ALL MEN

THURSDAY **APRIL 21**ST 2016	FRIDAY **APRIL 22**ND 2016	SATURDAY **APRIL 23**RD 2016
☐ I HAD MORNING PRAYER ☐ I HAD EVENING PRAYER	☐ I HAD MORNING PRAYER ☐ I HAD EVENING PRAYER	☐ I HAD MORNING PRAYER ☐ I HAD EVENING PRAYER

SIGNIFICANT THINGS THAT HAPPENED TODAY

SPECIFIC THINGS I DID TODAY TO PRESS FORWARD WITH A LOVE OF ALL MEN

GOAL(S) FOR TOMORROW TO PRESS FORWARD WITH A LOVE OF ALL MEN

SACRAMENT MEETING WHAT ARE SOME SPECIFIC LESSONS YOU LEARNED & IMPRESSIONS YOU HAD DURING SACRAMENT MEETING?

 CLASSES WHAT IMPORTANT DOCTRINES & PRINCIPLES DID YOU LEARN IN YOUR CLASSES?

Personal Progress

THIRD ADDITIONAL DIVINE NATURE EXPERIENCE

YOU MUST FULFILL 3 ADDITIONAL "DIVINE NATURE" EXPERIENCES. USE THIS PAGE TO COMPLETE ONE OF THE ADDITIONAL EXPERIENCES FOUND IN YOUR PERSONAL PROGRESS BOOK.

April 24-26

SUNDAY APRIL 24TH 2016	MONDAY APRIL 25TH 2016	TUESDAY APRIL 26TH 2016
☐ I HAD MORNING PRAYER ☐ I HAD EVENING PRAYER	☐ I HAD MORNING PRAYER ☐ I HAD EVENING PRAYER	☐ I HAD MORNING PRAYER ☐ I HAD EVENING PRAYER

SIGNIFICANT THINGS THAT HAPPENED TODAY

SPECIFIC THINGS I DID TODAY TO PRESS FORWARD WITH A LOVE OF ALL MEN

GOAL(S) FOR TOMORROW TO PRESS FORWARD WITH A LOVE OF ALL MEN

 april 27-29

PRESS FORWARD WITH A
LOVE OF ALL MEN

WEDNESDAY **APRIL 27**TH 2016	THURSDAY **APRIL 28**TH 2016	FRIDAY **APRIL 29**TH 2016
☐ I HAD MORNING PRAYER ☐ I HAD EVENING PRAYER	☐ I HAD MORNING PRAYER ☐ I HAD EVENING PRAYER	☐ I HAD MORNING PRAYER ☐ I HAD EVENING PRAYER

SIGNIFICANT THINGS THAT HAPPENED TODAY

SPECIFIC THINGS I DID TODAY TO PRESS FORWARD WITH A LOVE OF ALL MEN

GOAL(S) FOR TOMORROW TO PRESS FORWARD WITH A LOVE OF ALL MEN

SATURDAY **APRIL 30**TH 2016	SUNDAY **MAY 1**ST 2016	MONDAY **MAY 2**ND 2016
☐ I HAD MORNING PRAYER ☐ I HAD EVENING PRAYER	☐ I HAD MORNING PRAYER ☐ I HAD EVENING PRAYER	☐ I HAD MORNING PRAYER ☐ I HAD EVENING PRAYER

SIGNIFICANT THINGS THAT HAPPENED TODAY

SPECIFIC THINGS I DID TODAY TO PRESS FORWARD FEASTING UPON THE WORD OF CHRIST

GOAL(S) FOR TOMORROW TO PRESS FORWARD FEASTING UPON THE WORD OF CHRIST

The Sabbath Day
MAY 1ST

❦❦❦ SACRAMENT MEETING WHAT ARE SOME SPECIFIC LESSONS YOU LEARNED & IMPRESSIONS YOU HAD DURING SACRAMENT MEETING?

❦❦❦ CLASSES WHAT IMPORTANT DOCTRINES & PRINCIPLES DID YOU LEARN IN YOUR CLASSES?

HEAVENLY FATHER'S LOVE FOR YOU

You are a daughter of Heavenly Father, who knows you and loves you. Study the references below and doodle, draw, or diagram the things you learn from these scriptures. Particularly look for things that show how Heavenly Father knows you, loves you, and is mindful of you.

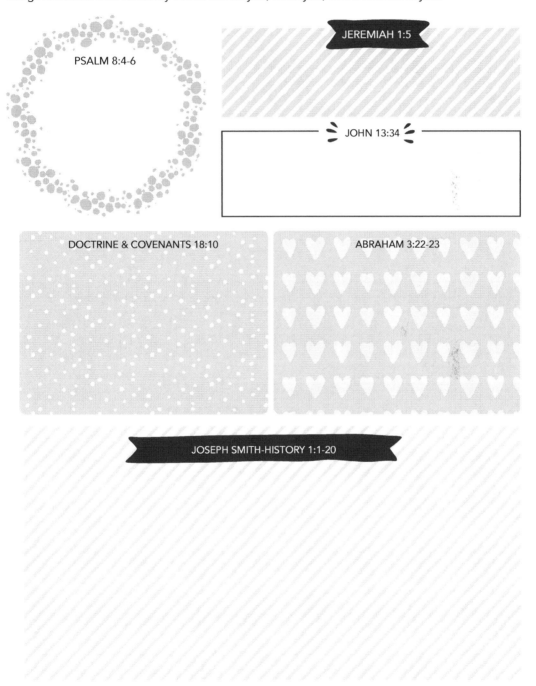

PSALM 8:4-6

JEREMIAH 1:5

JOHN 13:34

DOCTRINE & COVENANTS 18:10

ABRAHAM 3:22-23

JOSEPH SMITH-HISTORY 1:1-20

PRESS FORWARD FEASTING UPON THE WORD OF CHRIST

TUESDAY **MAY 3RD** 2016	WEDNESDAY **MAY 4TH** 2016	THURSDAY **MAY 5TH** 2016
☐ I HAD MORNING PRAYER ☐ I HAD EVENING PRAYER	☐ I HAD MORNING PRAYER ☐ I HAD EVENING PRAYER	☐ I HAD MORNING PRAYER ☐ I HAD EVENING PRAYER

SIGNIFICANT THINGS THAT HAPPENED TODAY

SPECIFIC THINGS I DID TODAY TO PRESS FORWARD FEASTING UPON THE WORD OF CHRIST

GOAL(S) FOR TOMORROW TO PRESS FORWARD FEASTING UPON THE WORD OF CHRIST

May 6-8

FRIDAY **MAY 6TH** 2016	SATURDAY **MAY 7TH** 2016	SUNDAY **MAY 8TH** 2016
☐ I HAD MORNING PRAYER ☐ I HAD EVENING PRAYER	☐ I HAD MORNING PRAYER ☐ I HAD EVENING PRAYER	☐ I HAD MORNING PRAYER ☐ I HAD EVENING PRAYER

SIGNIFICANT THINGS THAT HAPPENED TODAY

SPECIFIC THINGS I DID TODAY TO PRESS FORWARD FEASTING UPON THE WORD OF CHRIST

GOAL(S) FOR TOMORROW TO PRESS FORWARD FEASTING UPON THE WORD OF CHRIST

The Sabbath Day

MAY 8TH

✿✿✿SACRAMENT MEETING
WHAT ARE SOME SPECIFIC LESSONS YOU LEARNED & IMPRESSIONS YOU HAD DURING SACRAMENT MEETING?

✿✿✿CLASSES
WHAT IMPORTANT DOCTRINES & PRINCIPLES DID YOU LEARN IN YOUR CLASSES?

PATRIARCHAL BLESSINGS

Learn about the importance of patriarchal blessings by studying about them in True to the Faith and recent conference talks. Doodle, draw, or diagram the things you learn.

Discuss with a parent or Church leader how to prepare to receive a patriarchal blessing and how it can teach you of your worth and identity and be a guide throughout your life. Record what you learn.

If you have not yet received your Patriarchal Blessing, write down three things you can do to prepare to receive it.

ONE

TWO

THREE

MONDAY **MAY 9th** 2016	TUESDAY **MAY 10TH** 2016	WEDNESDAY **MAY 11TH** 2016
☐ I HAD MORNING PRAYER ☐ I HAD EVENING PRAYER	☐ I HAD MORNING PRAYER ☐ I HAD EVENING PRAYER	☐ I HAD MORNING PRAYER ☐ I HAD EVENING PRAYER

SIGNIFICANT THINGS THAT HAPPENED TODAY

SPECIFIC THINGS I DID TODAY TO PRESS FORWARD FEASTING UPON THE WORD OF CHRIST

GOAL(S) FOR TOMORROW TO PRESS FORWARD FEASTING UPON THE WORD OF CHRIST

May 12-14

THURSDAY **MAY 12**TH 2016	FRIDAY **MAY 13**TH 2016	SATURDAY **MAY 14**TH 2016
☐ I HAD MORNING PRAYER ☐ I HAD EVENING PRAYER	☐ I HAD MORNING PRAYER ☐ I HAD EVENING PRAYER	☐ I HAD MORNING PRAYER ☐ I HAD EVENING PRAYER

SIGNIFICANT THINGS THAT HAPPENED TODAY

SPECIFIC THINGS I DID TODAY TO PRESS FORWARD FEASTING UPON THE WORD OF CHRIST

GOAL(S) FOR TOMORROW TO PRESS FORWARD FEASTING UPON THE WORD OF CHRIST

The Sabbath Day

MAY 15TH

❦❦❦SACRAMENT MEETING
WHAT ARE SOME SPECIFIC LESSONS YOU LEARNED & IMPRESSIONS YOU HAD DURING SACRAMENT MEETING?

❦❦❦CLASSES
WHAT IMPORTANT DOCTRINES & PRINCIPLES DID YOU LEARN IN YOUR CLASSES?

THE INDIVIDUAL
WORTH OF OTHERS

Study Doctrine & Covenants 18:10 and 121:45. Doodle, write, or diagram what you learn about the individual worth of others.

Challenge: Every day for two weeks notice the worthwhile qualities and attributes of others. Acknowledge them verbally or in writing.

Brainstorm specific things you can do over the next two weeks to help make sure you notice worthwhile qualities and attributes of others.

May 15-17

PRESS FORWARD FEASTING
UPON THE WORD OF CHRIST

	SUNDAY MAY 15TH 2016	MONDAY MAY 16TH 2016	TUESDAY MAY 17TH 2016
	☐ I HAD MORNING PRAYER ☐ I HAD EVENING PRAYER	☐ I HAD MORNING PRAYER ☐ I HAD EVENING PRAYER	☐ I HAD MORNING PRAYER ☐ I HAD EVENING PRAYER
SIGNIFICANT THINGS THAT HAPPENED TODAY			
SPECIFIC THINGS I DID TODAY TO PRESS FORWARD FEASTING UPON THE WORD OF CHRIST			
GOAL(S) FOR TOMORROW TO PRESS FORWARD FEASTING UPON THE WORD OF CHRIST			
WORTHWHILE QUALITIES AND ATTRIBUTES I NOTICED IN OTHERS TODAY			

PRESS FORWARD FEASTING
UPON THE WORD OF CHRIST   🌷🌸🌷 *May 18-20* 🌷🌸🌷

WEDNESDAY MAY 18TH 2016	THURSDAY MAY 19TH 2016	FRIDAY MAY 20TH 2016
☐ I HAD MORNING PRAYER ☐ I HAD EVENING PRAYER	☐ I HAD MORNING PRAYER ☐ I HAD EVENING PRAYER	☐ I HAD MORNING PRAYER ☐ I HAD EVENING PRAYER

SIGNIFICANT THINGS THAT HAPPENED TODAY

SPECIFIC THINGS I DID TODAY TO PRESS FORWARD FEASTING UPON THE WORD OF CHRIST

GOAL(S) FOR TOMORROW TO PRESS FORWARD FEASTING UPON THE WORD OF CHRIST

WORTHWHILE QUALITIES AND ATTRIBUTES I NOTICED IN OTHERS TODAY

SATURDAY **MAY 21ST** 2016	SUNDAY **MAY 22ND** 2016	MONDAY **MAY 23RD** 2016
☐ I HAD MORNING PRAYER ☐ I HAD EVENING PRAYER	☐ I HAD MORNING PRAYER ☐ I HAD EVENING PRAYER	☐ I HAD MORNING PRAYER ☐ I HAD EVENING PRAYER

SIGNIFICANT THINGS THAT HAPPENED TODAY

SPECIFIC THINGS I DID TODAY TO PRESS FORWARD FEASTING UPON THE WORD OF CHRIST

GOAL(S) FOR TOMORROW TO PRESS FORWARD FEASTING UPON THE WORD OF CHRIST

WORTHWHILE QUALITIES AND ATTRIBUTES I NOTICED IN OTHERS TODAY

❧❧❧SACRAMENT MEETING
WHAT ARE SOME SPECIFIC LESSONS YOU LEARNED & IMPRESSIONS YOU HAD DURING SACRAMENT MEETING?

❧❧❧CLASSES
WHAT IMPORTANT DOCTRINES & PRINCIPLES DID YOU LEARN IN YOUR CLASSES?

THE INDIVIDUAL
WORTH OF OTHERS

What are some positive qualities you noticed in others this week that you may not have noticed if you were not doing this personal progress challenge?

How has noticing others' positive qualities impacted you?

What can you do to make this second week of the challenge more impactful than the first week?

TUESDAY **MAY 24**TH 2016	WEDNESDAY **MAY 25**TH 2016	THURSDAY **MAY 26**TH 2016	
☐ I HAD MORNING PRAYER ☐ I HAD EVENING PRAYER	☐ I HAD MORNING PRAYER ☐ I HAD EVENING PRAYER	☐ I HAD MORNING PRAYER ☐ I HAD EVENING PRAYER	
			SIGNIFICANT THINGS THAT HAPPENED TODAY
			SPECIFIC THINGS I DID TODAY TO PRESS FORWARD FEASTING UPON THE WORD OF CHRIST
			GOAL(S) FOR TOMORROW TO PRESS FORWARD FEASTING UPON THE WORD OF CHRIST
			WORTHWHILE QUALITIES AND ATTRIBUTES I NOTICED IN OTHERS TODAY

FRIDAY MAY 27TH 2016	SATURDAY MAY 28TH 2016	SUNDAY MAY 29TH 2016
□ I HAD MORNING PRAYER □ I HAD EVENING PRAYER	□ I HAD MORNING PRAYER □ I HAD EVENING PRAYER	□ I HAD MORNING PRAYER □ I HAD EVENING PRAYER

SIGNIFICANT THINGS THAT HAPPENED TODAY

SPECIFIC THINGS I DID TODAY TO PRESS FORWARD FEASTING UPON THE WORD OF CHRIST

GOAL(S) FOR TOMORROW TO PRESS FORWARD FEASTING UPON THE WORD OF CHRIST

WORTHWHILE QUALITIES AND ATTRIBUTES I NOTICED IN OTHERS TODAY

❀❀❀SACRAMENT MEETING WHAT ARE SOME SPECIFIC LESSONS YOU LEARNED & IMPRESSIONS YOU HAD DURING SACRAMENT MEETING?

❀❀❀CLASSES WHAT IMPORTANT DOCTRINES & PRINCIPLES DID YOU LEARN IN YOUR CLASSES?

Personal Progress

FIRST ADDITIONAL INDIVIDUAL WORTH EXPERIENCE

YOU MUST FULFILL 3 ADDITIONAL "INDIVIDUAL WORTH" EXPERIENCES. USE THIS PAGE TO COMPLETE ONE OF THE ADDITIONAL EXPERIENCES FOUND IN YOUR PERSONAL PROGRESS BOOK.

MONDAY **MAY 30**TH 2016	TUESDAY **MAY 31**ST 2016	WEDNESDAY **JUNE 1**ST 2016
☐ I HAD MORNING PRAYER ☐ I HAD EVENING PRAYER	☐ I HAD MORNING PRAYER ☐ I HAD EVENING PRAYER	☐ I HAD MORNING PRAYER ☐ I HAD EVENING PRAYER

SIGNIFICANT THINGS THAT HAPPENED TODAY

SPECIFIC THINGS I DID TODAY TO PRESS FORWARD FEASTING UPON THE WORD OF CHRIST

GOAL(S) FOR TOMORROW TO PRESS FORWARD FEASTING UPON THE WORD OF CHRIST

THURSDAY JUNE 2ND 2016	FRIDAY JUNE 3RD 2016	SATURDAY JUNE 4TH 2016
☐ I HAD MORNING PRAYER ☐ I HAD EVENING PRAYER	☐ I HAD MORNING PRAYER ☐ I HAD EVENING PRAYER	☐ I HAD MORNING PRAYER ☐ I HAD EVENING PRAYER

SIGNIFICANT THINGS THAT HAPPENED TODAY

SPECIFIC THINGS I DID TODAY TO PRESS FORWARD ENDURING TO THE END

GOAL(S) FOR TOMORROW TO PRESS FORWARD ENDURING TO THE END

SACRAMENT MEETING
WHAT ARE SOME SPECIFIC LESSONS YOU LEARNED & IMPRESSIONS YOU HAD DURING SACRAMENT MEETING?

CLASSES
WHAT IMPORTANT DOCTRINES & PRINCIPLES DID YOU LEARN IN YOUR CLASSES?

Personal Progress

SECOND ADDITIONAL INDIVIDUAL WORTH EXPERIENCE

YOU MUST FULFILL 3 ADDITIONAL "INDIVIDUAL WORTH" EXPERIENCES. USE THIS PAGE TO COMPLETE ONE OF THE ADDITIONAL EXPERIENCES FOUND IN YOUR PERSONAL PROGRESS BOOK.

SUNDAY JUNE 5TH 2016	MONDAY JUNE 6TH 2016	TUESDAY JUNE 7TH 2016
☐ I HAD MORNING PRAYER ☐ I HAD EVENING PRAYER	☐ I HAD MORNING PRAYER ☐ I HAD EVENING PRAYER	☐ I HAD MORNING PRAYER ☐ I HAD EVENING PRAYER

SIGNIFICANT THINGS THAT HAPPENED TODAY

SPECIFIC THINGS I DID TODAY TO PRESS FORWARD ENDURING TO THE END

GOAL(S) FOR TOMORROW TO PRESS FORWARD ENDURING TO THE END

WEDNESDAY JUNE 8TH 2016	THURSDAY JUNE 9TH 2016	FRIDAY JUNE 10TH 2016
☐ I HAD MORNING PRAYER ☐ I HAD EVENING PRAYER	☐ I HAD MORNING PRAYER ☐ I HAD EVENING PRAYER	☐ I HAD MORNING PRAYER ☐ I HAD EVENING PRAYER

SIGNIFICANT THINGS THAT HAPPENED TODAY

SPECIFIC THINGS I DID TODAY TO PRESS FORWARD ENDURING TO THE END

GOAL(S) FOR TOMORROW TO PRESS FORWARD ENDURING TO THE END

SATURDAY **JUNE 11**TH 2016	SUNDAY **JUNE 12**TH 2016	MONDAY **JUNE 13**TH 2016
☐ I HAD MORNING PRAYER ☐ I HAD EVENING PRAYER	☐ I HAD MORNING PRAYER ☐ I HAD EVENING PRAYER	☐ I HAD MORNING PRAYER ☐ I HAD EVENING PRAYER

SIGNIFICANT THINGS THAT HAPPENED TODAY

SPECIFIC THINGS I DID TODAY TO PRESS FORWARD ENDURING TO THE END

GOAL(S) FOR TOMORROW TO PRESS FORWARD ENDURING TO THE END

The Sabbath Day

❧ SACRAMENT MEETING ❧ WHAT ARE SOME SPECIFIC LESSONS YOU LEARNED & IMPRESSIONS YOU HAD DURING SACRAMENT MEETING?

❧ CLASSES ❧ WHAT IMPORTANT DOCTRINES & PRINCIPLES DID YOU LEARN IN YOUR CLASSES?

YOU MUST FULFILL 3 ADDITIONAL "INDIVIDUAL WORTH" EXPERIENCES. USE *Personal Progress*
THIS PAGE TO COMPLETE ONE OF THE ADDITIONAL EXPERIENCES FOUND IN
YOUR PERSONAL PROGRESS BOOK.

THIRD ADDITIONAL INDIVIDUAL WORTH EXPERIENCE

	TUESDAY JUNE 14TH 2016	WEDNESDAY JUNE 15TH 2016	THURSDAY JUNE 16TH 2016
	☐ I HAD MORNING PRAYER ☐ I HAD EVENING PRAYER	☐ I HAD MORNING PRAYER ☐ I HAD EVENING PRAYER	☐ I HAD MORNING PRAYER ☐ I HAD EVENING PRAYER
SIGNIFICANT THINGS THAT HAPPENED TODAY			
SPECIFIC THINGS I DID TODAY TO PRESS FORWARD ENDURING TO THE END			
GOAL(S) FOR TOMORROW TO PRESS FORWARD ENDURING TO THE END			

June 17-19

FRIDAY JUNE 17TH 2016	SATURDAY JUNE 18TH 2016	SUNDAY JUNE 19TH 2016
☐ I HAD MORNING PRAYER ☐ I HAD EVENING PRAYER	☐ I HAD MORNING PRAYER ☐ I HAD EVENING PRAYER	☐ I HAD MORNING PRAYER ☐ I HAD EVENING PRAYER

SIGNIFICANT THINGS THAT HAPPENED TODAY

SPECIFIC THINGS I DID TODAY TO PRESS FORWARD ENDURING TO THE END

GOAL(S) FOR TOMORROW TO PRESS FORWARD ENDURING TO THE END

The Sabbath Day
JUNE 19th

SACRAMENT MEETING
WHAT ARE SOME SPECIFIC LESSONS YOU LEARNED & IMPRESSIONS YOU HAD DURING SACRAMENT MEETING?

CLASSES
WHAT IMPORTANT DOCTRINES & PRINCIPLES DID YOU LEARN IN YOUR CLASSES?

- PROVERBS 1:5
- PROVERBS 4:7
- 2 NEPHI 28:30
- DOCTRINE & COVENANTS 88:78-80
- DOCTRINE & COVENANTS 88:118
- DOCTRINE & COVENANTS 90:15
- DOCTRINE & COVENANTS 130:18-19
- DOCTRINE & COVENANTS 131:6

IMPORTANCE OF GAINING KNOWLEDGE

Learn about the importance of gaining knowledge by studying the scriptures above. Diagram, doodle, or record what you learn as you study the scriptures.

Why do you need to gain knowledge about how to apply gospel principles to your present and future home and family life?

Ask a parent or leader for advice on specific things you can do to gain knowledge about how to apply gospel principles to your present and future life. Record what you learn below.

June 20-22   PRESS FORWARD ENDURING TO THE END

MONDAY JUNE 20TH 2016	TUESDAY JUNE 21ST 2016	WEDNESDAY JUNE 22ND 2016
☐ I HAD MORNING PRAYER ☐ I HAD EVENING PRAYER	☐ I HAD MORNING PRAYER ☐ I HAD EVENING PRAYER	☐ I HAD MORNING PRAYER ☐ I HAD EVENING PRAYER

SIGNIFICANT THINGS THAT HAPPENED TODAY

SPECIFIC THINGS I DID TODAY TO PRESS FORWARD ENDURING TO THE END

GOAL(S) FOR TOMORROW TO PRESS FORWARD ENDURING TO THE END

THURSDAY JUNE 23RD 2016	FRIDAY JUNE 24TH 2016	SATURDAY JUNE 25TH 2016
□ I HAD MORNING PRAYER □ I HAD EVENING PRAYER	□ I HAD MORNING PRAYER □ I HAD EVENING PRAYER	□ I HAD MORNING PRAYER □ I HAD EVENING PRAYER

SIGNIFICANT THINGS THAT HAPPENED TODAY

SPECIFIC THINGS I DID TODAY TO PRESS FORWARD ENDURING TO THE END

GOAL(S) FOR TOMORROW TO PRESS FORWARD ENDURING TO THE END

The Sabbath Day
JUNE 26th

⚜ SACRAMENT MEETING ⚜
WHAT ARE SOME SPECIFIC LESSONS YOU LEARNED &
IMPRESSIONS YOU HAD DURING SACRAMENT MEETING?

⚜ CLASSES ⚜
WHAT IMPORTANT DOCTRINES & PRINCIPLES DID YOU LEARN IN YOUR CLASSES?

SKILLS & TALENTS

Make a list of talents and skills you currently have (ask your parents and grandparents for insight into talents they have observed in you.).

Make a list of talents and skills you would like to develop.

Matthew 25:14-30 What do these scriptures teach you about the importance of developing your own talents?

Make a list of talents or skills you can develop that will help you care for your future family and home.

Pick one of the talents or skills that you would like to develop that will help you care for your future family and home. Make a plan on specific things you can do to develop that talent or skill.

SUNDAY **JUNE 26**TH 2016	MONDAY **JUNE 27**TH 2016	TUESDAY **JUNE 28**TH 2016
☐ I HAD MORNING PRAYER ☐ I HAD EVENING PRAYER	☐ I HAD MORNING PRAYER ☐ I HAD EVENING PRAYER	☐ I HAD MORNING PRAYER ☐ I HAD EVENING PRAYER

SIGNIFICANT THINGS THAT HAPPENED TODAY

SPECIFIC THINGS I DID TODAY TO PRESS FORWARD ENDURING TO THE END

GOAL(S) FOR TOMORROW TO PRESS FORWARD ENDURING TO THE END

WEDNESDAY **JUNE 29TH** 2016	THURSDAY **JUNE 30TH** 2016	FRIDAY **JULY 1ST** 2016
☐ I HAD MORNING PRAYER ☐ I HAD EVENING PRAYER	☐ I HAD MORNING PRAYER ☐ I HAD EVENING PRAYER	☐ I HAD MORNING PRAYER ☐ I HAD EVENING PRAYER

SIGNIFICANT THINGS THAT HAPPENED TODAY

SPECIFIC THINGS I DID TODAY TO PRESS FORWARD ENDURING TO THE END

GOAL(S) FOR TOMORROW TO PRESS FORWARD ENDURING TO THE END

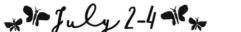 July 2-4

PRESS FORWARD WITH A STEADFASTNESS IN CHRIST

SATURDAY JULY 2nd 2016	SUNDAY JULY 3RD 2016	MONDAY JULY 4TH 2016
☐ I HAD MORNING PRAYER ☐ I HAD EVENING PRAYER	☐ I HAD MORNING PRAYER ☐ I HAD EVENING PRAYER	☐ I HAD MORNING PRAYER ☐ I HAD EVENING PRAYER

SIGNIFICANT THINGS THAT HAPPENED TODAY

SPECIFIC THINGS I DID TODAY TO PRESS FORWARD WITH STEADFASTNESS IN CHRIST

GOAL(S) FOR TOMORROW TO PRESS FORWARD WITH STEADFASTNESS IN CHRIST

SACRAMENT MEETING
WHAT ARE SOME SPECIFIC LESSONS YOU LEARNED & IMPRESSIONS YOU HAD DURING SACRAMENT MEETING?

CLASSES
WHAT IMPORTANT DOCTRINES & PRINCIPLES DID YOU LEARN IN YOUR CLASSES?

Article of faith #13

We believe in being honest, true, chaste, benevolent, virtuous, and in doing good to all men; indeed, we may say that we follow the admonition of Paul—We believe all things, we hope all things, we have endured many things, and hope to be able to endure all things. If there is anything virtuous, lovely, or of good report or praiseworthy, we seek after these things.

Memorize Article of Faith #13. When you have done so, check the box below.

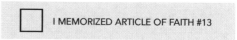

☐ I MEMORIZED ARTICLE OF FAITH #13

This week, visit a museum or exhibit or attend a performance that involves dance, music, speech, or drama. Using this article of faith as a guide, evaluate what you saw and heard and write about it below.

How can you use this article of faith as a guide for all you do so the Holy Ghost will be your constant companion?

PRESS FORWARD WITH A STEADFASTNESS IN CHRIST

 July 5-7

TUESDAY JULY 5TH 2016	WEDNESDAY JULY 6TH 2016	THURSDAY JULY 7TH 2016
☐ I HAD MORNING PRAYER ☐ I HAD EVENING PRAYER	☐ I HAD MORNING PRAYER ☐ I HAD EVENING PRAYER	☐ I HAD MORNING PRAYER ☐ I HAD EVENING PRAYER

SIGNIFICANT THINGS THAT HAPPENED TODAY

SPECIFIC THINGS I DID TODAY TO PRESS FORWARD WITH STEADFASTNESS IN CHRIST

GOAL(S) FOR TOMORROW TO PRESS FORWARD WITH STEADFASTNESS IN CHRIST

July 8-10

PRESS FORWARD WITH A STEADFASTNESS IN CHRIST

FRIDAY **JULY 8**TH 2016	SATURDAY **JULY 9**TH 2016	SUNDAY **JULY 10**TH 2016
☐ I HAD MORNING PRAYER ☐ I HAD EVENING PRAYER	☐ I HAD MORNING PRAYER ☐ I HAD EVENING PRAYER	☐ I HAD MORNING PRAYER ☐ I HAD EVENING PRAYER

SIGNIFICANT THINGS THAT HAPPENED TODAY

SPECIFIC THINGS I DID TODAY TO PRESS FORWARD WITH STEADFASTNESS IN CHRIST

GOAL(S) FOR TOMORROW TO PRESS FORWARD WITH STEADFASTNESS IN CHRIST

SACRAMENT MEETING
WHAT ARE SOME SPECIFIC LESSONS YOU LEARNED & IMPRESSIONS YOU HAD DURING SACRAMENT MEETING?

CLASSES
WHAT IMPORTANT DOCTRINES & PRINCIPLES DID YOU LEARN IN YOUR CLASSES?

Personal Progress

YOU MUST FULFILL 3 ADDITIONAL "KNOWLEDGE" EXPERIENCES. USE THIS PAGE TO COMPLETE ONE OF THE ADDITIONAL EXPERIENCES FOUND IN YOUR PERSONAL PROGRESS BOOK.

MONDAY JULY 11TH 2016	TUESDAY JULY 12TH 2016	WEDNESDAY JULY 13TH 2016
☐ I HAD MORNING PRAYER ☐ I HAD EVENING PRAYER	☐ I HAD MORNING PRAYER ☐ I HAD EVENING PRAYER	☐ I HAD MORNING PRAYER ☐ I HAD EVENING PRAYER

SIGNIFICANT THINGS THAT HAPPENED TODAY

SPECIFIC THINGS I DID TODAY TO PRESS FORWARD WITH STEADFASTNESS IN CHRIST

GOAL(S) FOR TOMORROW TO PRESS FORWARD WITH STEADFASTNESS IN CHRIST

THURSDAY **JULY 14**TH 2016	FRIDAY **JULY 15**TH 2016	SATURDAY **JULY 16**TH 2016
☐ I HAD MORNING PRAYER ☐ I HAD EVENING PRAYER	☐ I HAD MORNING PRAYER ☐ I HAD EVENING PRAYER	☐ I HAD MORNING PRAYER ☐ I HAD EVENING PRAYER

SIGNIFICANT THINGS THAT HAPPENED TODAY

SPECIFIC THINGS I DID TODAY TO PRESS FORWARD WITH STEADFASTNESS IN CHRIST

GOAL(S) FOR TOMORROW TO PRESS FORWARD WITH STEADFASTNESS IN CHRIST

SACRAMENT MEETING
WHAT ARE SOME SPECIFIC LESSONS YOU LEARNED & IMPRESSIONS YOU HAD DURING SACRAMENT MEETING?

CLASSES
WHAT IMPORTANT DOCTRINES & PRINCIPLES DID YOU LEARN IN YOUR CLASSES?

Personal Progress

SECOND ADDITIONAL KNOWLEDGE EXPERIENCE

YOU MUST FULFILL 3 ADDITIONAL "KNOWLEDGE" EXPERIENCES. USE THIS PAGE TO COMPLETE ONE OF THE ADDITIONAL EXPERIENCES FOUND IN YOUR PERSONAL PROGRESS BOOK.

SUNDAY **JULY 17**TH 2016	MONDAY **JULY 18**TH 2016	TUESDAY **JULY 19**TH 2016
□ I HAD MORNING PRAYER □ I HAD EVENING PRAYER	□ I HAD MORNING PRAYER □ I HAD EVENING PRAYER	□ I HAD MORNING PRAYER □ I HAD EVENING PRAYER

SIGNIFICANT THINGS THAT HAPPENED TODAY

SPECIFIC THINGS I DID TODAY TO PRESS FORWARD WITH STEADFASTNESS IN CHRIST

GOAL(S) FOR TOMORROW TO PRESS FORWARD WITH STEADFASTNESS IN CHRIST

WEDNESDAY **JULY 20**TH 2016	THURSDAY **JULY 21**ST 2016	FRIDAY **JULY 22**ND 2016
☐ I HAD MORNING PRAYER ☐ I HAD EVENING PRAYER	☐ I HAD MORNING PRAYER ☐ I HAD EVENING PRAYER	☐ I HAD MORNING PRAYER ☐ I HAD EVENING PRAYER

SIGNIFICANT THINGS THAT HAPPENED TODAY

SPECIFIC THINGS I DID TODAY TO PRESS FORWARD WITH STEADFASTNESS IN CHRIST

GOAL(S) FOR TOMORROW TO PRESS FORWARD WITH STEADFASTNESS IN CHRIST

SATURDAY **JULY 23**RD 2016	SUNDAY **JULY 24**TH 2016	MONDAY **JULY 25**TH 2016
☐ I HAD MORNING PRAYER ☐ I HAD EVENING PRAYER	☐ I HAD MORNING PRAYER ☐ I HAD EVENING PRAYER	☐ I HAD MORNING PRAYER ☐ I HAD EVENING PRAYER

SIGNIFICANT THINGS THAT HAPPENED TODAY

SPECIFIC THINGS I DID TODAY TO PRESS FORWARD WITH STEADFASTNESS IN CHRIST

GOAL(S) FOR TOMORROW TO PRESS FORWARD WITH STEADFASTNESS IN CHRIST

The Sabbath Day

JULY 24TH

SACRAMENT MEETING

WHAT ARE SOME SPECIFIC LESSONS YOU LEARNED & IMPRESSIONS YOU HAD DURING SACRAMENT MEETING?

CLASSES

WHAT IMPORTANT DOCTRINES & PRINCIPLES DID YOU LEARN IN YOUR CLASSES?

YOU MUST FULFILL 3 ADDITIONAL "KNOWLEDGE" EXPERIENCES. USE *Personal Progress*
THIS PAGE TO COMPLETE ONE OF THE ADDITIONAL EXPERIENCES
FOUND IN YOUR PERSONAL PROGRESS BOOK.

THIRD ADDITIONAL KNOWLEDGE EXPERIENCE

TUESDAY JULY 26TH 2016	WEDNESDAY JULY 27TH 2016	THURSDAY JULY 28TH 2016
☐ I HAD MORNING PRAYER ☐ I HAD EVENING PRAYER	☐ I HAD MORNING PRAYER ☐ I HAD EVENING PRAYER	☐ I HAD MORNING PRAYER ☐ I HAD EVENING PRAYER

SIGNIFICANT THINGS THAT HAPPENED TODAY

SPECIFIC THINGS I DID TODAY TO PRESS FORWARD WITH STEADFASTNESS IN CHRIST

GOAL(S) FOR TOMORROW TO PRESS FORWARD WITH STEADFASTNESS IN CHRIST

FRIDAY **JULY 29**TH 2016	SATURDAY **JULY 30**TH 2016	SUNDAY **JULY 31**ST 2016
☐ I HAD MORNING PRAYER ☐ I HAD EVENING PRAYER	☐ I HAD MORNING PRAYER ☐ I HAD EVENING PRAYER	☐ I HAD MORNING PRAYER ☐ I HAD EVENING PRAYER

SIGNIFICANT THINGS THAT HAPPENED TODAY

SPECIFIC THINGS I DID TODAY TO PRESS FORWARD WITH STEADFASTNESS IN CHRIST

GOAL(S) FOR TOMORROW TO PRESS FORWARD WITH STEADFASTNESS IN CHRIST

The Sabbath Day
JULY 31ST

SACRAMENT MEETING
WHAT ARE SOME SPECIFIC LESSONS YOU LEARNED & IMPRESSIONS YOU HAD DURING SACRAMENT MEETING?

CLASSES
WHAT IMPORTANT DOCTRINES & PRINCIPLES DID YOU LEARN IN YOUR CLASSES?

1 Nephi 15: 8
2 Nephi 32: 3
Alma 34: 19-27
Ether 2-3
D&C 9: 7-9

I CAN MAKE WISE DECISIONS & SOLVE PROBLEMS

A daughter of God can make wise decisions and solve problems. Read the above scriptures and doodle, write about, or diagram what you learn about making wise choices and solving problems.

Follow a pattern of regular scripture study and prayer to receive help in making personal decisions such as choosing good friends, being kind to others, getting up on time, or other decisions. What can you do to make sure you implement a pattern of regular scripture study and prayer?

In what ways do you think establishing this pattern in your life will make a difference in the kind of choices you make?

MONDAY AUGUST 1ST 2016	TUESDAY AUGUST 2ND 2016	WEDNESDAY AUGUST 3RD 2016
☐ I HAD MORNING PRAYER ☐ I HAD EVENING PRAYER	☐ I HAD MORNING PRAYER ☐ I HAD EVENING PRAYER	☐ I HAD MORNING PRAYER ☐ I HAD EVENING PRAYER
☐ I STUDIED THE SCRIPTURES	☐ I STUDIED THE SCRIPTURES	☐ I STUDIED THE SCRIPTURES

SIGNIFICANT THINGS THAT HAPPENED TODAY

SPECIFIC THINGS I DID TODAY TO PRESS FORWARD WITH A PERFECT BRIGHTNESS OF HOPE

GOAL(S) FOR TOMORROW TO PRESS FORWARD WITH A PERFECT BRIGHTNESS OF HOPE

THURSDAY **AUGUST 4**TH 2016	FRIDAY **AUGUST 5**TH 2016	SATURDAY **AUGUST 6**TH 2016
☐ I HAD MORNING PRAYER ☐ I HAD EVENING PRAYER	☐ I HAD MORNING PRAYER ☐ I HAD EVENING PRAYER	☐ I HAD MORNING PRAYER ☐ I HAD EVENING PRAYER
☐ I STUDIED THE SCRIPTURES	☐ I STUDIED THE SCRIPTURES	☐ I STUDIED THE SCRIPTURES

SIGNIFICANT THINGS THAT HAPPENED TODAY

SPECIFIC THINGS I DID TODAY TO PRESS FORWARD WITH A PERFECT BRIGHTNESS OF HOPE

GOAL(S) FOR TOMORROW TO PRESS FORWARD WITH A PERFECT BRIGHTNESS OF HOPE

The Sabbath Day

 SACRAMENT MEETING WHAT ARE SOME SPECIFIC LESSONS YOU LEARNED & IMPRESSIONS YOU HAD DURING SACRAMENT MEETING?

CLASSES  WHAT IMPORTANT DOCTRINES & PRINCIPLES DID YOU LEARN IN YOUR CLASSES?

Personal Progress

CHOICE & ACCOUNTABILITY EXPERIENCE #2
(THREE WEEK EXPERIENCE)

I CAN LIVE THE LORD'S STANDARDS

Read about each standard in the *For the Strength of Youth* pamphlet. Next to each standard write one of the promises you will receive when you live that standard.

STANDARD	PROMISE
AGENCY & ACCOUNTABILITY	
DATING	
DRESS & APPEARANCE	
EDUCATION	
ENTERTAINMENT & MEDIA	
FAMILY	
FRIENDS	
GRATITUDE	
HONESTY & INTEGRITY	
LANGUAGE	
MUSIC & DANCING	
PHYSICAL & EMOTIONAL HEALTH	
REPENTANCE	
SABBATH DAY OBSERVANCE	
SERVICE	
SEXUAL PURITY	
TITHES & OFFERINGS	
WORK & SELF-RELIANCE	

Challenge: Choose three standards in which you need to improve. Work on improving those standards over the next three weeks. Record the standards you chose below.

ONE	TWO	THREE

August 7-9

SUNDAY **AUGUST 7TH** 2016	MONDAY **AUGUST 8TH** 2016	TUESDAY **AUGUST 9TH** 2016
□ I HAD MORNING PRAYER □ I HAD EVENING PRAYER	□ I HAD MORNING PRAYER □ I HAD EVENING PRAYER	□ I HAD MORNING PRAYER □ I HAD EVENING PRAYER
□ I STUDIED THE SCRIPTURES	□ I STUDIED THE SCRIPTURES	□ I STUDIED THE SCRIPTURES

SIGNIFICANT THINGS THAT HAPPENED TODAY

SPECIFIC THINGS I DID TODAY TO PRESS FORWARD WITH A PERFECT BRIGHTNESS OF HOPE

GOAL(S) FOR TOMORROW TO PRESS FORWARD WITH A PERFECT BRIGHTNESS OF HOPE

3 STANDARDS CHALLENGE: HOW DID IT GO TODAY?

STANDARD #1	STANDARD #1	STANDARD #1
STANDARD #2	STANDARD #2	STANDARD #2
STANDARD #3	STANDARD #3	STANDARD #3

 *August 10-12*

WEDNESDAY **AUGUST 10TH** 2016	THURSDAY **AUGUST 11TH** 2016	FRIDAY **AUGUST 12TH** 2016
☐ I HAD MORNING PRAYER ☐ I HAD EVENING PRAYER ☐ I STUDIED THE SCRIPTURES	☐ I HAD MORNING PRAYER ☐ I HAD EVENING PRAYER ☐ I STUDIED THE SCRIPTURES	☐ I HAD MORNING PRAYER ☐ I HAD EVENING PRAYER ☐ I STUDIED THE SCRIPTURES

SIGNIFICANT THINGS THAT HAPPENED TODAY

SPECIFIC THINGS I DID TODAY TO PRESS FORWARD WITH A PERFECT BRIGHTNESS OF HOPE

GOAL(S) FOR TOMORROW TO PRESS FORWARD WITH A PERFECT BRIGHTNESS OF HOPE

3 STANDARDS CHALLENGE: HOW DID IT GO TODAY?

STANDARD #1	STANDARD #1	STANDARD #1
STANDARD #2	STANDARD #2	STANDARD #2
STANDARD #3	STANDARD #3	STANDARD #3

PRESS FORWARD WITH A PERFECT BRIGHTNESS OF HOPE

SATURDAY AUGUST 13TH 2016	SUNDAY AUGUST 14TH 2016	MONDAY AUGUST 15TH 2016
□ I HAD MORNING PRAYER □ I HAD EVENING PRAYER	□ I HAD MORNING PRAYER □ I HAD EVENING PRAYER	□ I HAD MORNING PRAYER □ I HAD EVENING PRAYER
□ I STUDIED THE SCRIPTURES	□ I STUDIED THE SCRIPTURES	□ I STUDIED THE SCRIPTURES

SIGNIFICANT THINGS THAT HAPPENED TODAY

SPECIFIC THINGS I DID TODAY TO PRESS FORWARD WITH A PERFECT BRIGHTNESS OF HOPE

GOAL(S) FOR TOMORROW TO PRESS FORWARD WITH A PERFECT BRIGHTNESS OF HOPE

3 STANDARDS CHALLENGE: HOW DID IT GO TODAY?

STANDARD #1	STANDARD #1	STANDARD #1
STANDARD #2	STANDARD #2	STANDARD #2
STANDARD #3	STANDARD #3	STANDARD #3

SACRAMENT MEETING  WHAT ARE SOME SPECIFIC LESSONS YOU LEARNED & IMPRESSIONS YOU HAD DURING SACRAMENT MEETING?

CLASSES WHAT IMPORTANT DOCTRINES & PRINCIPLES DID YOU LEARN IN YOUR CLASSES?

I CAN LIVE THE
LORD'S STANDARDS

What difference have you noticed in your life as you have sought to live the three standards you chose to focus on last week?

Take some time and study the three standards in *For the Strength of Youth.* In the spaces below record things that stand out to you as you study each standard.

STANDARD #1

STANDARD #2

STANDARD #3

PRESS FORWARD WITH A
PERFECT BRIGHTNESS OF HOPE

August 16-18

TUESDAY AUGUST 16TH 2016	WEDNESDAY AUGUST 17TH 2016	THURSDAY AUGUST 18TH 2016	
☐ I HAD MORNING PRAYER ☐ I HAD EVENING PRAYER ☐ I STUDIED THE SCRIPTURES	☐ I HAD MORNING PRAYER ☐ I HAD EVENING PRAYER ☐ I STUDIED THE SCRIPTURES	☐ I HAD MORNING PRAYER ☐ I HAD EVENING PRAYER ☐ I STUDIED THE SCRIPTURES	
			SIGNIFICANT THINGS THAT HAPPENED TODAY
			SPECIFIC THINGS I DID TODAY TO PRESS FORWARD WITH A PERFECT BRIGHTNESS OF HOPE
			GOAL(S) FOR TOMORROW TO PRESS FORWARD WITH A PERFECT BRIGHTNESS OF HOPE
STANDARD #1	STANDARD #1	STANDARD #1	3 STANDARDS CHALLENGE: HOW DID IT GO TODAY?
STANDARD #2	STANDARD #2	STANDARD #2	
STANDARD #3	STANDARD #3	STANDARD #3	

FRIDAY AUGUST 19TH 2016	SATURDAY AUGUST 20TH 2016	SUNDAY AUGUST 21ST 2016
☐ I HAD MORNING PRAYER ☐ I HAD EVENING PRAYER	☐ I HAD MORNING PRAYER ☐ I HAD EVENING PRAYER	☐ I HAD MORNING PRAYER ☐ I HAD EVENING PRAYER
☐ I STUDIED THE SCRIPTURES	☐ I STUDIED THE SCRIPTURES	☐ I STUDIED THE SCRIPTURES

SIGNIFICANT THINGS THAT HAPPENED TODAY

SPECIFIC THINGS I DID TODAY TO PRESS FORWARD WITH A PERFECT BRIGHTNESS OF HOPE

GOAL(S) FOR TOMORROW TO PRESS FORWARD WITH A PERFECT BRIGHTNESS OF HOPE

3 STANDARDS CHALLENGE: HOW DID IT GO TODAY?

STANDARD #1	STANDARD #1	STANDARD #1
STANDARD #2	STANDARD #2	STANDARD #2
STANDARD #3	STANDARD #3	STANDARD #3

 SACRAMENT MEETING   WHAT ARE SOME SPECIFIC LESSONS YOU LEARNED & IMPRESSIONS YOU HAD DURING SACRAMENT MEETING?

 CLASSES WHAT IMPORTANT DOCTRINES & PRINCIPLES DID YOU LEARN IN YOUR CLASSES?

Personal Progress

I CAN LIVE THE LORD'S STANDARDS

What difference have you noticed in your life as you have sought to live the three standards you chose to focus on last week?

Study the three standards in *For the Strength of Youth* again. In the spaces below, record promises you are given as you live these standards. Include your own testimony and thoughts.

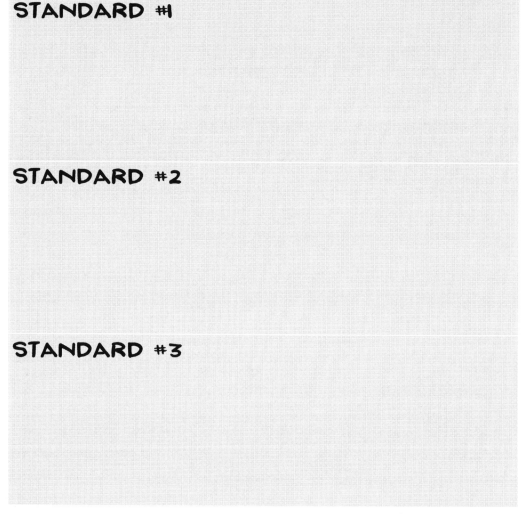

STANDARD #1

STANDARD #2

STANDARD #3

PRESS FORWARD WITH A
PERFECT BRIGHTNESS OF HOPE

 August 22-24

MONDAY AUGUST 22ND 2016	TUESDAY AUGUST 23RD 2016	WEDNESDAY AUGUST 24TH 2016
□ I HAD MORNING PRAYER □ I HAD EVENING PRAYER	□ I HAD MORNING PRAYER □ I HAD EVENING PRAYER	□ I HAD MORNING PRAYER □ I HAD EVENING PRAYER
□ I STUDIED THE SCRIPTURES	□ I STUDIED THE SCRIPTURES	□ I STUDIED THE SCRIPTURES

SIGNIFICANT THINGS THAT HAPPENED TODAY

SPECIFIC THINGS I DID TODAY TO PRESS FORWARD WITH A PERFECT BRIGHTNESS OF HOPE

GOAL(S) FOR TOMORROW TO PRESS FORWARD WITH A PERFECT BRIGHTNESS OF HOPE

3 STANDARDS CHALLENGE: HOW DID IT GO TODAY?

STANDARD #1	STANDARD #1	STANDARD #1
STANDARD #2	STANDARD #2	STANDARD #2
STANDARD #3	STANDARD #3	STANDARD #3

August 25-27

PRESS FORWARD WITH A PERFECT BRIGHTNESS OF HOPE

THURSDAY AUGUST 25TH 2016	FRIDAY AUGUST 26TH 2016	SATURDAY AUGUST 27TH 2016
□ I HAD MORNING PRAYER □ I HAD EVENING PRAYER □ I STUDIED THE SCRIPTURES	□ I HAD MORNING PRAYER □ I HAD EVENING PRAYER □ I STUDIED THE SCRIPTURES	□ I HAD MORNING PRAYER □ I HAD EVENING PRAYER □ I STUDIED THE SCRIPTURES

SIGNIFICANT THINGS THAT HAPPENED TODAY

SPECIFIC THINGS I DID TODAY TO PRESS FORWARD WITH A PERFECT BRIGHTNESS OF HOPE

GOAL(S) FOR TOMORROW TO PRESS FORWARD WITH A PERFECT BRIGHTNESS OF HOPE

3 STANDARDS CHALLENGE: HOW DID IT GO TODAY?

STANDARD #1	STANDARD #1	STANDARD #1
STANDARD #2	STANDARD #2	STANDARD #2
STANDARD #3	STANDARD #3	STANDARD #3

The Sabbath Day

AUGUST 28TH

🦉 SACRAMENT MEETING 🦉 WHAT ARE SOME SPECIFIC LESSONS YOU LEARNED & IMPRESSIONS YOU HAD DURING SACRAMENT MEETING?

🦉 CLASSES 🦉 WHAT IMPORTANT DOCTRINES & PRINCIPLES DID YOU LEARN IN YOUR CLASSES?

UNDERSTANDING
AGENCY

Agency, or the ability to choose, is one of God's greatest gifts to His children. Read about agency in the following scriptures. Doodle or write what you learn from each scripture.

JOSHUA 24:15

2 NEPHI 2

DOCTRINE & COVENANTS 82:2-10

With a parent or leader, discuss the blessings and responsibilities of agency. Below, record your understanding of agency and the consequences of choices and actions.

PRESS FORWARD WITH A
PERFECT BRIGHTNESS OF HOPE

 August 28-30

SUNDAY AUGUST 28TH 2016	MONDAY AUGUST 29TH 2016	TUESDAY AUGUST 30TH 2016
☐ I HAD MORNING PRAYER ☐ I HAD EVENING PRAYER	☐ I HAD MORNING PRAYER ☐ I HAD EVENING PRAYER	☐ I HAD MORNING PRAYER ☐ I HAD EVENING PRAYER
☐ I STUDIED THE SCRIPTURES	☐ I STUDIED THE SCRIPTURES	☐ I STUDIED THE SCRIPTURES

SIGNIFICANT THINGS THAT HAPPENED TODAY

SPECIFIC THINGS I DID TODAY TO PRESS FORWARD WITH A PERFECT BRIGHTNESS OF HOPE

GOAL(S) FOR TOMORROW TO PRESS FORWARD WITH A PERFECT BRIGHTNESS OF HOPE

PRESS FORWARD WITH A LOVE OF GOD

WEDNESDAY AUGUST 31ST 2016	THURSDAY SEPTEMBER 1ST 2016	FRIDAY SEPTEMBER 2ND 2016
☐ I HAD MORNING PRAYER ☐ I HAD EVENING PRAYER	☐ I HAD MORNING PRAYER ☐ I HAD EVENING PRAYER	☐ I HAD MORNING PRAYER ☐ I HAD EVENING PRAYER
☐ I STUDIED THE SCRIPTURES	☐ I STUDIED THE SCRIPTURES	☐ I STUDIED THE SCRIPTURES

SIGNIFICANT THINGS THAT HAPPENED TODAY

SPECIFIC THINGS I DID TODAY TO PRESS FORWARD WITH A LOVE OF GOD

GOAL(S) FOR TOMORROW TO PRESS FORWARD WITH A LOVE OF GOD

September 3-5

SATURDAY **SEPTEMBER 3RD** 2016	SUNDAY **SEPTEMBER 4TH** 2016	MONDAY **SEPTEMBER 5TH** 2016
☐ I HAD MORNING PRAYER ☐ I HAD EVENING PRAYER	☐ I HAD MORNING PRAYER ☐ I HAD EVENING PRAYER	☐ I HAD MORNING PRAYER ☐ I HAD EVENING PRAYER
☐ I STUDIED THE SCRIPTURES	☐ I STUDIED THE SCRIPTURES	☐ I STUDIED THE SCRIPTURES

SIGNIFICANT THINGS THAT HAPPENED TODAY

SPECIFIC THINGS I DID TODAY TO PRESS FORWARD WITH A LOVE OF GOD

GOAL(S) FOR TOMORROW TO PRESS FORWARD WITH A LOVE OF GOD

The Sabbath Day

SEPTEMBER 4TH

SACRAMENT MEETING
WHAT ARE SOME SPECIFIC LESSONS YOU LEARNED & IMPRESSIONS YOU HAD DURING SACRAMENT MEETING?

CLASSES
WHAT IMPORTANT DOCTRINES & PRINCIPLES DID YOU LEARN IN YOUR CLASSES?

YOU MUST FULFILL 3 ADDITIONAL "CHOICE & ACCOUNTABILITY" EXPERIENCES. USE THIS PAGE TO COMPLETE ONE OF THE ADDITIONAL EXPERIENCES FOUND IN YOUR PERSONAL PROGRESS BOOK.

Personal Progress

FIRST ADDITIONAL CHOICE & ACCOUNTABILITY EXPERIENCE

TUESDAY SEPTEMBER 6TH 2016	WEDNESDAY SEPTEMBER 7TH 2016	THURSDAY SEPTEMBER 8TH 2016
☐ I HAD MORNING PRAYER ☐ I HAD EVENING PRAYER	☐ I HAD MORNING PRAYER ☐ I HAD EVENING PRAYER	☐ I HAD MORNING PRAYER ☐ I HAD EVENING PRAYER
☐ I STUDIED THE SCRIPTURES	☐ I STUDIED THE SCRIPTURES	☐ I STUDIED THE SCRIPTURES

SIGNIFICANT THINGS THAT HAPPENED TODAY

SPECIFIC THINGS I DID TODAY TO PRESS FORWARD WITH A LOVE OF GOD

GOAL(S) FOR TOMORROW TO PRESS FORWARD WITH A LOVE OF GOD

September 9-11

FRIDAY SEPTEMBER 9TH 2016	SATURDAY SEPTEMBER 10TH 2016	SUNDAY SEPTEMBER 11TH 2016
☐ I HAD MORNING PRAYER ☐ I HAD EVENING PRAYER	☐ I HAD MORNING PRAYER ☐ I HAD EVENING PRAYER	☐ I HAD MORNING PRAYER ☐ I HAD EVENING PRAYER
☐ I STUDIED THE SCRIPTURES	☐ I STUDIED THE SCRIPTURES	☐ I STUDIED THE SCRIPTURES

SIGNIFICANT THINGS THAT HAPPENED TODAY

SPECIFIC THINGS I DID TODAY TO PRESS FORWARD WITH A LOVE OF GOD

GOAL(S) FOR TOMORROW TO PRESS FORWARD WITH A LOVE OF GOD

The Sabbath Day

SEPTEMBER 11TH

SACRAMENT MEETING
WHAT ARE SOME SPECIFIC LESSONS YOU LEARNED &
IMPRESSIONS YOU HAD DURING SACRAMENT MEETING?

CLASSES
WHAT IMPORTANT DOCTRINES & PRINCIPLES DID YOU LEARN IN YOUR CLASSES?

YOU MUST FULFILL 3 ADDITIONAL "CHOICE & ACCOUNTABILITY" EXPERIENCES. USE THIS PAGE TO COMPLETE ONE OF THE ADDITIONAL EXPERIENCES FOUND IN YOUR PERSONAL PROGRESS BOOK.

Personal Progress

SECOND ADDITIONAL CHOICE & ACCOUNTABILITY EXPERIENCE

September 12-14

MONDAY SEPTEMBER 12TH 2016	TUESDAY SEPTEMBER 13TH 2016	WEDNESDAY SEPTEMBER 14TH 2016
☐ I HAD MORNING PRAYER ☐ I HAD EVENING PRAYER	☐ I HAD MORNING PRAYER ☐ I HAD EVENING PRAYER	☐ I HAD MORNING PRAYER ☐ I HAD EVENING PRAYER
☐ I STUDIED THE SCRIPTURES	☐ I STUDIED THE SCRIPTURES	☐ I STUDIED THE SCRIPTURES

SIGNIFICANT THINGS THAT HAPPENED TODAY

SPECIFIC THINGS I DID TODAY TO PRESS FORWARD WITH A LOVE OF GOD

GOAL(S) FOR TOMORROW TO PRESS FORWARD WITH A LOVE OF GOD

THURSDAY SEPTEMBER 15TH 2016	FRIDAY SEPTEMBER 16TH 2016	SATURDAY SEPTEMBER 17TH 2016
☐ I HAD MORNING PRAYER ☐ I HAD EVENING PRAYER	☐ I HAD MORNING PRAYER ☐ I HAD EVENING PRAYER	☐ I HAD MORNING PRAYER ☐ I HAD EVENING PRAYER
☐ I STUDIED THE SCRIPTURES	☐ I STUDIED THE SCRIPTURES	☐ I STUDIED THE SCRIPTURES

SIGNIFICANT THINGS THAT HAPPENED TODAY

SPECIFIC THINGS I DID TODAY TO PRESS FORWARD WITH A LOVE OF GOD

GOAL(S) FOR TOMORROW TO PRESS FORWARD WITH A LOVE OF GOD

The Sabbath Day

SEPTEMBER 18TH

SACRAMENT MEETING
WHAT ARE SOME SPECIFIC LESSONS YOU LEARNED & IMPRESSIONS YOU HAD DURING SACRAMENT MEETING?

CLASSES
WHAT IMPORTANT DOCTRINES & PRINCIPLES DID YOU LEARN IN YOUR CLASSES?

YOU MUST FULFILL 3 ADDITIONAL "CHOICE & ACCOUNTABILITY" EXPERIENCES. USE THIS PAGE TO COMPLETE ONE OF THE ADDITIONAL EXPERIENCES FOUND IN YOUR PERSONAL PROGRESS BOOK.

Personal Progress

THIRD ADDITIONAL CHOICE & ACCOUNTABILITY EXPERIENCE

September 18-20

PRESS FORWARD WITH A LOVE OF GOD

SUNDAY **SEPTEMBER 18**TH 2016	MONDAY **SEPTEMBER 19**TH 2016	TUESDAY **SEPTEMBER 20**TH 2016
☐ I HAD MORNING PRAYER ☐ I HAD EVENING PRAYER	☐ I HAD MORNING PRAYER ☐ I HAD EVENING PRAYER	☐ I HAD MORNING PRAYER ☐ I HAD EVENING PRAYER
☐ I STUDIED THE SCRIPTURES	☐ I STUDIED THE SCRIPTURES	☐ I STUDIED THE SCRIPTURES

SIGNIFICANT THINGS THAT HAPPENED TODAY

SPECIFIC THINGS I DID TODAY TO PRESS FORWARD WITH A LOVE OF GOD

GOAL(S) FOR TOMORROW TO PRESS FORWARD WITH A LOVE OF GOD

WEDNESDAY SEPTEMBER 21ST 2016	THURSDAY SEPTEMBER 22ND 2016	FRIDAY SEPTEMBER 23RD 2016
☐ I HAD MORNING PRAYER ☐ I HAD EVENING PRAYER	☐ I HAD MORNING PRAYER ☐ I HAD EVENING PRAYER	☐ I HAD MORNING PRAYER ☐ I HAD EVENING PRAYER
☐ I STUDIED THE SCRIPTURES	☐ I STUDIED THE SCRIPTURES	☐ I STUDIED THE SCRIPTURES

SIGNIFICANT THINGS THAT HAPPENED TODAY

SPECIFIC THINGS I DID TODAY TO PRESS FORWARD WITH A LOVE OF GOD

GOAL(S) FOR TOMORROW TO PRESS FORWARD WITH A LOVE OF GOD

SATURDAY SEPTEMBER 24TH 2016	SUNDAY SEPTEMBER 25TH 2016	MONDAY SEPTEMBER 26TH 2016
☐ I HAD MORNING PRAYER ☐ I HAD EVENING PRAYER	☐ I HAD MORNING PRAYER ☐ I HAD EVENING PRAYER	☐ I HAD MORNING PRAYER ☐ I HAD EVENING PRAYER
☐ I STUDIED THE SCRIPTURES	☐ I STUDIED THE SCRIPTURES	☐ I STUDIED THE SCRIPTURES

SIGNIFICANT THINGS THAT HAPPENED TODAY

SPECIFIC THINGS I DID TODAY TO PRESS FORWARD WITH A LOVE OF GOD

GOAL(S) FOR TOMORROW TO PRESS FORWARD WITH A LOVE OF GOD

The Sabbath Day

SEPTEMBER 25TH

❧ SACRAMENT MEETING ❧ WHAT ARE SOME SPECIFIC LESSONS YOU LEARNED & IMPRESSIONS YOU HAD DURING SACRAMENT MEETING?

❧ CLASSES ❧ WHAT IMPORTANT DOCTRINES & PRINCIPLES DID YOU LEARN IN YOUR CLASSES?

Personal Progress

SERVICE:
A FUNDAMENTAL GOSPEL PRINCIPLE

Learn why service is a fundamental principle of the gospel. Doodle, diagram, or write what each scripture teaches you about service.

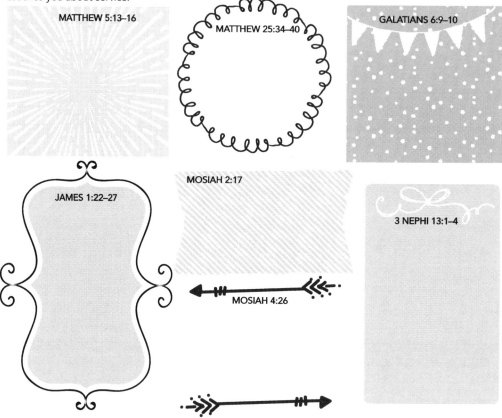

MATTHEW 5:13–16

MATTHEW 25:34–40

GALATIANS 6:9–10

JAMES 1:22–27

MOSIAH 2:17

3 NEPHI 13:1–4

MOSIAH 4:26

Challenge:

Others often give service you may not notice, such as preparing meals, reading to or listening to younger children, repairing clothing, or helping a brother or sister.

For two weeks, record in your journal the quiet acts of service your family members and others perform. Acknowledge their service in some meaningful way.

PRESS FORWARD WITH A LOVE OF GOD

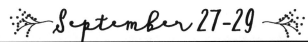

September 27-29

TUESDAY SEPTEMBER 27TH 2016	WEDNESDAY SEPTEMBER 28TH 2016	THURSDAY SEPTEMBER 29TH 2016
☐ I HAD MORNING PRAYER ☐ I HAD EVENING PRAYER	☐ I HAD MORNING PRAYER ☐ I HAD EVENING PRAYER	☐ I HAD MORNING PRAYER ☐ I HAD EVENING PRAYER
☐ I STUDIED THE SCRIPTURES	☐ I STUDIED THE SCRIPTURES	☐ I STUDIED THE SCRIPTURES

SIGNIFICANT THINGS THAT HAPPENED TODAY

SPECIFIC THINGS I DID TODAY TO PRESS FORWARD WITH A LOVE OF GOD

GOAL(S) FOR TOMORROW TO PRESS FORWARD WITH A LOVE OF GOD

QUIET ACTS OF SERVICE I SAW OTHERS PERFORM TODAY

FRIDAY SEPTEMBER 30TH 2016	SATURDAY OCTOBER 1ST 2016	SUNDAY OCTOBER 2ND 2016
☐ I HAD MORNING PRAYER ☐ I HAD EVENING PRAYER	☐ I HAD MORNING PRAYER ☐ I HAD EVENING PRAYER	☐ I HAD MORNING PRAYER ☐ I HAD EVENING PRAYER
☐ I STUDIED THE SCRIPTURES	☐ I STUDIED THE SCRIPTURES	☐ I STUDIED THE SCRIPTURES

SIGNIFICANT THINGS THAT HAPPENED TODAY

SPECIFIC THINGS I DID TODAY TO PRESS FORWARD WITH A LOVE OF ALL MEN

GOAL(S) FOR TOMORROW TO PRESS FORWARD WITH A LOVE OF ALL MEN

QUIET ACTS OF SERVICE I SAW OTHERS PERFORM TODAY

General Conference
OCTOBER 2ND

LESSONS LEARNED
WHAT LESSONS STOOD OUT TO YOU MOST DURING GENERAL CONFERENCE?

PERSONAL GOALS
WHAT PERSONAL GOALS WOULD YOU LIKE TO MAKE BECAUSE OF WHAT YOU LEARNED?

How have you been impacted this week as you noticed the service others quietly performed? What have you learned?

"GOD DOES NOTICE US, AND HE WATCHES OVER US. BUT IT IS USUALLY THROUGH ANOTHER PERSON THAT HE MEETS OUR NEEDS."

President Spencer W. Kimball

Read the quote above. What are some things you have observed this past week that are examples of the teaching in this quote?

 *October 3-5*

MONDAY **OCTOBER 3RD** 2016	TUESDAY **OCTOBER 4TH** 2016	WEDNESDAY **OCTOBER 5TH** 2016
☐ I HAD MORNING PRAYER ☐ I HAD EVENING PRAYER	☐ I HAD MORNING PRAYER ☐ I HAD EVENING PRAYER	☐ I HAD MORNING PRAYER ☐ I HAD EVENING PRAYER
☐ I STUDIED THE SCRIPTURES	☐ I STUDIED THE SCRIPTURES	☐ I STUDIED THE SCRIPTURES

SIGNIFICANT THINGS THAT HAPPENED TODAY

SPECIFIC THINGS I DID TODAY TO PRESS FORWARD WITH A LOVE OF ALL MEN

GOAL(S) FOR TOMORROW TO PRESS FORWARD WITH A LOVE OF ALL MEN

QUIET ACTS OF SERVICE I SAW OTHERS PERFORM TODAY

PRESS FORWARD WITH A
LOVE OF ALL MEN

THURSDAY OCTOBER 6TH 2016	FRIDAY OCTOBER 7TH 2016	SATURDAY OCTOBER 8TH 2016
☐ I HAD MORNING PRAYER ☐ I HAD EVENING PRAYER	☐ I HAD MORNING PRAYER ☐ I HAD EVENING PRAYER	☐ I HAD MORNING PRAYER ☐ I HAD EVENING PRAYER
☐ I STUDIED THE SCRIPTURES	☐ I STUDIED THE SCRIPTURES	☐ I STUDIED THE SCRIPTURES

SIGNIFICANT THINGS THAT HAPPENED TODAY

SPECIFIC THINGS I DID TODAY TO PRESS FORWARD WITH A LOVE OF ALL MEN

GOAL(S) FOR TOMORROW TO PRESS FORWARD WITH A LOVE OF ALL MEN

QUIET ACTS OF SERVICE I SAW OTHERS PERFORM TODAY

The Sabbath Day

OCTOBER 9TH

SACRAMENT MEETING

WHAT ARE SOME SPECIFIC LESSONS YOU LEARNED & IMPRESSIONS YOU HAD DURING SACRAMENT MEETING?

CLASSES

WHAT IMPORTANT DOCTRINES & PRINCIPLES DID YOU LEARN IN YOUR CLASSES?

Personal Progress

GOOD WORKS EXPERIENCE #2
(2 WEEK EXPERIENCE)

FAMILY MEALS

Service is an essential principle of family living.

Two Week Challenge:

- ☑ Help plan your family's menus
- ☑ Help obtain the food
- ☑ Prepare part of the meals for two weeks
- ☑ Help your family gather to share mealtimes

FAMILY MENU

	BREAKFAST	LUNCH	DINNER
MONDAY			
TUESDAY			
WEDNESDAY			
THURSDAY			
FRIDAY			
SATURDAY			
SUNDAY			

 October 9-11

SUNDAY OCTOBER 9TH 2016	MONDAY OCTOBER 10TH 2016	TUESDAY OCTOBER 11TH 2016
□ I HAD MORNING PRAYER □ I HAD EVENING PRAYER	□ I HAD MORNING PRAYER □ I HAD EVENING PRAYER	□ I HAD MORNING PRAYER □ I HAD EVENING PRAYER
□ I STUDIED THE SCRIPTURES	□ I STUDIED THE SCRIPTURES	□ I STUDIED THE SCRIPTURES

SIGNIFICANT THINGS THAT HAPPENED TODAY

SPECIFIC THINGS I DID TODAY TO PRESS FORWARD WITH A LOVE OF ALL MEN

GOAL(S) FOR TOMORROW TO PRESS FORWARD WITH A LOVE OF ALL MEN

WHAT I DID TO HELP WITH FAMILY MEALS

October 12-14

WEDNESDAY **OCTOBER 12TH** 2016	THURSDAY **OCTOBER 13TH** 2016	FRIDAY **OCTOBER 14TH** 2016
☐ I HAD MORNING PRAYER ☐ I HAD EVENING PRAYER	☐ I HAD MORNING PRAYER ☐ I HAD EVENING PRAYER	☐ I HAD MORNING PRAYER ☐ I HAD EVENING PRAYER
☐ I STUDIED THE SCRIPTURES	☐ I STUDIED THE SCRIPTURES	☐ I STUDIED THE SCRIPTURES

SIGNIFICANT THINGS THAT HAPPENED TODAY

SPECIFIC THINGS I DID TODAY TO PRESS FORWARD WITH A LOVE OF ALL MEN

GOAL(S) FOR TOMORROW TO PRESS FORWARD WITH A LOVE OF ALL MEN

WHAT I DID TO HELP WITH FAMILY MEALS

October 15-17

SATURDAY OCTOBER 15TH 2016	SUNDAY OCTOBER 16TH 2016	MONDAY OCTOBER 17TH 2016
□ I HAD MORNING PRAYER □ I HAD EVENING PRAYER	□ I HAD MORNING PRAYER □ I HAD EVENING PRAYER	□ I HAD MORNING PRAYER □ I HAD EVENING PRAYER
□ I STUDIED THE SCRIPTURES	□ I STUDIED THE SCRIPTURES	□ I STUDIED THE SCRIPTURES

SIGNIFICANT THINGS THAT HAPPENED TODAY

SPECIFIC THINGS I DID TODAY TO PRESS FORWARD WITH A LOVE OF ALL MEN

GOAL(S) FOR TOMORROW TO PRESS FORWARD WITH A LOVE OF ALL MEN

WHAT I DID TO HELP WITH FAMILY MEALS

The Sabbath Day

OCTOBER 16TH

🎃 SACRAMENT MEETING 🎃

WHAT ARE SOME SPECIFIC LESSONS YOU LEARNED &
IMPRESSIONS YOU HAD DURING SACRAMENT MEETING?

🎃 CLASSES 🎃

WHAT IMPORTANT DOCTRINES & PRINCIPLES DID YOU LEARN IN YOUR CLASSES?

FAMILY MEALS

Personal Progress

GOOD WORKS EXPERIENCE #2
(2 WEEK EXPERIENCE)

As you continue to help with family meals this next week, what can you do to help make family mealtime extra special and meaningful for your family?

FAMILY MENU

	BREAKFAST	LUNCH	DINNER
MONDAY			
TUESDAY			
WEDNESDAY			
THURSDAY			
FRIDAY			
SATURDAY			
SUNDAY			

PRESS FORWARD WITH A
LOVE OF ALL MEN

	TUESDAY OCTOBER 18TH 2016	WEDNESDAY OCTOBER 19TH 2016	THURSDAY OCTOBER 20TH 2016
	□ I HAD MORNING PRAYER □ I HAD EVENING PRAYER	□ I HAD MORNING PRAYER □ I HAD EVENING PRAYER	□ I HAD MORNING PRAYER □ I HAD EVENING PRAYER
	□ I STUDIED THE SCRIPTURES	□ I STUDIED THE SCRIPTURES	□ I STUDIED THE SCRIPTURES
SIGNIFICANT THINGS THAT HAPPENED TODAY			
SPECIFIC THINGS I DID TODAY TO PRESS FORWARD WITH A LOVE OF ALL MEN			
GOAL(S) FOR TOMORROW TO PRESS FORWARD WITH A LOVE OF ALL MEN			
WHAT I DID TO HELP WITH FAMILY MEALS			

 October 21-23

FRIDAY OCTOBER 21ST 2016	SATURDAY OCTOBER 22ND 2016	SUNDAY OCTOBER 23RD 2016
☐ I HAD MORNING PRAYER ☐ I HAD EVENING PRAYER	☐ I HAD MORNING PRAYER ☐ I HAD EVENING PRAYER	☐ I HAD MORNING PRAYER ☐ I HAD EVENING PRAYER
☐ I STUDIED THE SCRIPTURES	☐ I STUDIED THE SCRIPTURES	☐ I STUDIED THE SCRIPTURES

SIGNIFICANT THINGS THAT HAPPENED TODAY

SPECIFIC THINGS I DID TODAY TO PRESS FORWARD WITH A LOVE OF ALL MEN

GOAL(S) FOR TOMORROW TO PRESS FORWARD WITH A LOVE OF ALL MEN

WHAT I DID TO HELP WITH FAMILY MEALS

The Sabbath Day

OCTOBER 23RD

🎃 SACRAMENT MEETING 🎃
WHAT ARE SOME SPECIFIC LESSONS YOU LEARNED & IMPRESSIONS YOU HAD DURING SACRAMENT MEETING?

🎃 CLASSES 🎃
WHAT IMPORTANT DOCTRINES & PRINCIPLES DID YOU LEARN IN YOUR CLASSES?

COMFORTING OTHERS

Mosiah 18:7-10 explains what you promised to do when you were baptized. Using those verses, fill in the blanks below:

AT BAPTISM I PROMISED TO:

1 BEAR ONE ANOTHER'S _____, THAT THEY MAY BE _____.

2 WILLING TO _____ WITH THOSE THAT _____.

3 TO _____ THOSE THAT STAND IN NEED OF _____.

How would it bless everyone if every member of the church did all they could to keep this baptismal covenant?

What are three things you could do this week to keep the baptismal covenant above?

ONE:

TWO:

THREE

 October 24-26

PRESS FORWARD WITH A
LOVE OF ALL MEN

MONDAY OCTOBER 24TH 2016	TUESDAY OCTOBER 25TH 2016	WEDNESDAY OCTOBER 26TH 2016
☐ I HAD MORNING PRAYER ☐ I HAD EVENING PRAYER	☐ I HAD MORNING PRAYER ☐ I HAD EVENING PRAYER	☐ I HAD MORNING PRAYER ☐ I HAD EVENING PRAYER
☐ I STUDIED THE SCRIPTURES	☐ I STUDIED THE SCRIPTURES	☐ I STUDIED THE SCRIPTURES

SIGNIFICANT THINGS THAT HAPPENED TODAY

SPECIFIC THINGS I DID TODAY TO PRESS FORWARD WITH A LOVE OF ALL MEN

GOAL(S) FOR TOMORROW TO PRESS FORWARD WITH A LOVE OF ALL MEN

WHAT I DID TODAY TO KEEP MY BAPTISMAL COVENANT

THURSDAY OCTOBER 27TH 2016	FRIDAY OCTOBER 28TH 2016	SATURDAY OCTOBER 29TH 2016
☐ I HAD MORNING PRAYER ☐ I HAD EVENING PRAYER	☐ I HAD MORNING PRAYER ☐ I HAD EVENING PRAYER	☐ I HAD MORNING PRAYER ☐ I HAD EVENING PRAYER
☐ I STUDIED THE SCRIPTURES	☐ I STUDIED THE SCRIPTURES	☐ I STUDIED THE SCRIPTURES

SIGNIFICANT THINGS THAT HAPPENED TODAY

SPECIFIC THINGS I DID TODAY TO PRESS FORWARD WITH A LOVE OF ALL MEN

GOAL(S) FOR TOMORROW TO PRESS FORWARD WITH A LOVE OF ALL MEN

WHAT I DID TODAY TO KEEP MY BAPTISMAL COVENANT

The Sabbath Day
OCTOBER 30TH

🎃 SACRAMENT MEETING 🎃 WHAT ARE SOME SPECIFIC LESSONS YOU LEARNED & IMPRESSIONS YOU HAD DURING SACRAMENT MEETING?

🎃 CLASSES 🎃 WHAT IMPORTANT DOCTRINES & PRINCIPLES DID YOU LEARN IN YOUR CLASSES?

YOU MUST FULFILL 3 ADDITIONAL "GOOD WORKS" EXPERIENCES.
USE THIS PAGE TO COMPLETE ONE OF THE ADDITIONAL EXPERIENCES
FOUND IN YOUR PERSONAL PROGRESS BOOK.

Personal Progress
FIRST ADDITIONAL GOOD WORKS EXPERIENCE

PRESS FORWARD WITH A LOVE OF ALL MEN

SUNDAY **OCTOBER 30**TH 2016	MONDAY **OCTOBER 31**ST 2016	TUESDAY **NOVEMBER 1**ST 2016
□ I HAD MORNING PRAYER □ I HAD EVENING PRAYER	□ I HAD MORNING PRAYER □ I HAD EVENING PRAYER	□ I HAD MORNING PRAYER □ I HAD EVENING PRAYER
□ I STUDIED THE SCRIPTURES	□ I STUDIED THE SCRIPTURES	□ I STUDIED THE SCRIPTURES

SIGNIFICANT THINGS THAT HAPPENED TODAY

SPECIFIC THINGS I DID TODAY TO PRESS FORWARD WITH A LOVE OF ALL MEN

GOAL(S) FOR TOMORROW TO PRESS FORWARD WITH A LOVE OF ALL MEN

November 2-4

WEDNESDAY NOVEMBER 2ND 2016	THURSDAY NOVEMBER 3RD 2016	FRIDAY NOVEMBER 4TH 2016
☐ I HAD MORNING PRAYER ☐ I HAD EVENING PRAYER	☐ I HAD MORNING PRAYER ☐ I HAD EVENING PRAYER	☐ I HAD MORNING PRAYER ☐ I HAD EVENING PRAYER
☐ I STUDIED THE SCRIPTURES	☐ I STUDIED THE SCRIPTURES	☐ I STUDIED THE SCRIPTURES

SIGNIFICANT THINGS THAT HAPPENED TODAY

SPECIFIC THINGS I DID TODAY TO PRESS FORWARD FEASTING UPON THE WORD OF CHRIST

GOAL(S) FOR TOMORROW TO PRESS FORWARD FEASTING UPON THE WORD OF CHRIST

November 5-7

SATURDAY NOVEMBER 5TH 2016	SUNDAY NOVEMBER 6TH 2016	MONDAY NOVEMBER 7TH 2016
☐ I HAD MORNING PRAYER ☐ I HAD EVENING PRAYER	☐ I HAD MORNING PRAYER ☐ I HAD EVENING PRAYER	☐ I HAD MORNING PRAYER ☐ I HAD EVENING PRAYER
☐ I STUDIED THE SCRIPTURES	☐ I STUDIED THE SCRIPTURES	☐ I STUDIED THE SCRIPTURES

SIGNIFICANT THINGS THAT HAPPENED TODAY

SPECIFIC THINGS I DID TODAY TO PRESS FORWARD FEASTING UPON THE WORD OF CHRIST

GOAL(S) FOR TOMORROW TO PRESS FORWARD FEASTING UPON THE WORD OF CHRIST

SACRAMENT MEETING  WHAT ARE SOME SPECIFIC LESSONS YOU LEARNED &
IMPRESSIONS YOU HAD DURING SACRAMENT MEETING?

CLASSES WHAT IMPORTANT DOCTRINES & PRINCIPLES DID YOU LEARN IN YOUR CLASSES?

Personal Progress

SECOND ADDITIONAL GOOD WORKS EXPERIENCE

YOU MUST FULFILL 3 ADDITIONAL "GOOD WORKS" EXPERIENCES. USE THIS PAGE TO COMPLETE ONE OF THE ADDITIONAL EXPERIENCES FOUND IN YOUR PERSONAL PROGRESS BOOK.

TUESDAY NOVEMBER 8TH 2016	WEDNESDAY NOVEMBER 9TH 2016	THURSDAY NOVEMBER 10TH 2016
☐ I HAD MORNING PRAYER ☐ I HAD EVENING PRAYER	☐ I HAD MORNING PRAYER ☐ I HAD EVENING PRAYER	☐ I HAD MORNING PRAYER ☐ I HAD EVENING PRAYER
☐ I STUDIED THE SCRIPTURES	☐ I STUDIED THE SCRIPTURES	☐ I STUDIED THE SCRIPTURES

SIGNIFICANT THINGS THAT HAPPENED TODAY

SPECIFIC THINGS I DID TODAY TO PRESS FORWARD FEASTING UPON THE WORD OF CHRIST

GOAL(S) FOR TOMORROW TO PRESS FORWARD FEASTING UPON THE WORD OF CHRIST

FRIDAY **NOVEMBER 11**TH 2016	SATURDAY **NOVEMBER 12**TH 2016	SUNDAY **NOVEMBER 13**TH 2016
☐ I HAD MORNING PRAYER ☐ I HAD EVENING PRAYER	☐ I HAD MORNING PRAYER ☐ I HAD EVENING PRAYER	☐ I HAD MORNING PRAYER ☐ I HAD EVENING PRAYER
☐ I STUDIED THE SCRIPTURES	☐ I STUDIED THE SCRIPTURES	☐ I STUDIED THE SCRIPTURES

SIGNIFICANT THINGS THAT HAPPENED TODAY

SPECIFIC THINGS I DID TODAY TO PRESS FORWARD FEASTING UPON THE WORD OF CHRIST

GOAL(S) FOR TOMORROW TO PRESS FORWARD FEASTING UPON THE WORD OF CHRIST

SACRAMENT MEETING

WHAT ARE SOME SPECIFIC LESSONS YOU LEARNED &
IMPRESSIONS YOU HAD DURING SACRAMENT MEETING?

CLASSES

WHAT IMPORTANT DOCTRINES & PRINCIPLES DID YOU LEARN IN YOUR CLASSES?

Personal Progress

THIRD ADDITIONAL GOOD WORKS EXPERIENCE

YOU MUST FULFILL 3 ADDITIONAL "GOOD WORKS" EXPERIENCES. USE THIS PAGE TO COMPLETE ONE OF THE ADDITIONAL EXPERIENCES FOUND IN YOUR PERSONAL PROGRESS BOOK.

MONDAY NOVEMBER 14TH 2016	TUESDAY NOVEMBER 15TH 2016	WEDNESDAY NOVEMBER 16TH 2016
□ I HAD MORNING PRAYER □ I HAD EVENING PRAYER	□ I HAD MORNING PRAYER □ I HAD EVENING PRAYER	□ I HAD MORNING PRAYER □ I HAD EVENING PRAYER
□ I STUDIED THE SCRIPTURES	□ I STUDIED THE SCRIPTURES	□ I STUDIED THE SCRIPTURES

SIGNIFICANT THINGS THAT HAPPENED TODAY

SPECIFIC THINGS I DID TODAY TO PRESS FORWARD FEASTING UPON THE WORD OF CHRIST

GOAL(S) FOR TOMORROW TO PRESS FORWARD FEASTING UPON THE WORD OF CHRIST

November 17-19

PRESS FORWARD FEASTING
UPON THE WORD OF CHRIST

THURSDAY NOVEMBER 17TH 2016	FRIDAY NOVEMBER 18TH 2016	SATURDAY NOVEMBER 19TH 2016
☐ I HAD MORNING PRAYER ☐ I HAD EVENING PRAYER	☐ I HAD MORNING PRAYER ☐ I HAD EVENING PRAYER	☐ I HAD MORNING PRAYER ☐ I HAD EVENING PRAYER
☐ I STUDIED THE SCRIPTURES	☐ I STUDIED THE SCRIPTURES	☐ I STUDIED THE SCRIPTURES

SIGNIFICANT THINGS THAT HAPPENED TODAY

SPECIFIC THINGS I DID TODAY TO PRESS FORWARD FEASTING UPON THE WORD OF CHRIST

GOAL(S) FOR TOMORROW TO PRESS FORWARD FEASTING UPON THE WORD OF CHRIST

The Sabbath Day

NOVEMBER 20TH

SACRAMENT MEETING

WHAT ARE SOME SPECIFIC LESSONS YOU LEARNED &
IMPRESSIONS YOU HAD DURING SACRAMENT MEETING?

CLASSES

WHAT IMPORTANT DOCTRINES & PRINCIPLES DID YOU LEARN IN YOUR CLASSES?

Personal Progress

INTEGRITY EXPERIENCE #1
(ONE MONTH CHALLENGE)

WHAT IS INTEGRITY?

Integrity is the willingness and desire to live by our beliefs and standards. Study Moroni 10:30–33 and write your thoughts about what it means to "deny yourselves of all ungodliness."

>>> DENYING MYSELF OF ALL UNGODLINESS MEANS...<<<

Using *For the Strength of Youth*, record what the Lord's standards are for all of the below topics.

	THE LORD'S STANDARDS
HOW I DRESS	
MY CONVERSATIONS	
MY BEHAVIOR	
LITERATURE I READ	
MOVIES I WATCH	
TELEVISION I WATCH	
HOW I USE THE INTERNET	
MUSIC I LISTEN TO	
HOW I USE MY CELL PHONE	
BEING SEXUALLY PURE	

Challenge: If you have "integrity", then you are willing to live what you believe. This means that you will live the Lord's standards, like the ones you wrote about above. For one month, report to yourself every day on how you did on living up to the standards you wrote about above.

SUNDAY NOVEMBER 20TH 2016	MONDAY NOVEMBER 21ST 2016	TUESDAY NOVEMBER 22ND 2016
□ I HAD MORNING PRAYER □ I HAD EVENING PRAYER	□ I HAD MORNING PRAYER □ I HAD EVENING PRAYER	□ I HAD MORNING PRAYER □ I HAD EVENING PRAYER
□ I STUDIED THE SCRIPTURES	□ I STUDIED THE SCRIPTURES	□ I STUDIED THE SCRIPTURES

SIGNIFICANT THINGS THAT HAPPENED TODAY

SPECIFIC THINGS I DID TODAY TO PRESS FORWARD FEASTING UPON THE WORD OF CHRIST

GOAL(S) FOR TOMORROW TO PRESS FORWARD FEASTING UPON THE WORD OF CHRIST

INTEGRITY: WHAT I DID TODAY TO LIVE UP TO THE LORD'S STANDARDS

November 23-25

PRESS FORWARD FEASTING UPON THE WORD OF CHRIST

	WEDNESDAY **NOVEMBER 23RD** 2016	THURSDAY **NOVEMBER 24TH** 2016	FRIDAY **NOVEMBER 25TH** 2016
	☐ I HAD MORNING PRAYER ☐ I HAD EVENING PRAYER	☐ I HAD MORNING PRAYER ☐ I HAD EVENING PRAYER	☐ I HAD MORNING PRAYER ☐ I HAD EVENING PRAYER
	☐ I STUDIED THE SCRIPTURES	☐ I STUDIED THE SCRIPTURES	☐ I STUDIED THE SCRIPTURES
SIGNIFICANT THINGS THAT HAPPENED TODAY			
SPECIFIC THINGS I DID TODAY TO PRESS FORWARD FEASTING UPON THE WORD OF CHRIST			
GOAL(S) FOR TOMORROW TO PRESS FORWARD FEASTING UPON THE WORD OF CHRIST			
INTEGRITY: WHAT I DID TODAY TO LIVE UP TO THE LORD'S STANDARDS			

SATURDAY NOVEMBER 26TH 2016	SUNDAY NOVEMBER 27TH 2016	MONDAY NOVEMBER 28TH 2016
☐ I HAD MORNING PRAYER ☐ I HAD EVENING PRAYER	☐ I HAD MORNING PRAYER ☐ I HAD EVENING PRAYER	☐ I HAD MORNING PRAYER ☐ I HAD EVENING PRAYER
☐ I STUDIED THE SCRIPTURES	☐ I STUDIED THE SCRIPTURES	☐ I STUDIED THE SCRIPTURES

SIGNIFICANT THINGS THAT HAPPENED TODAY

SPECIFIC THINGS I DID TODAY TO PRESS FORWARD FEASTING UPON THE WORD OF CHRIST

GOAL(S) FOR TOMORROW TO PRESS FORWARD FEASTING UPON THE WORD OF CHRIST

INTEGRITY: WHAT I DID TODAY TO LIVE UP TO THE LORD'S STANDARDS

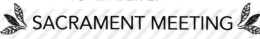

The Sabbath Day

NOVEMBER 27TH

SACRAMENT MEETING

WHAT ARE SOME SPECIFIC LESSONS YOU LEARNED & IMPRESSIONS YOU HAD DURING SACRAMENT MEETING?

CLASSES

WHAT IMPORTANT DOCTRINES & PRINCIPLES DID YOU LEARN IN YOUR CLASSES?

WHAT IS INTEGRITY?

What experiences, challenges, and blessings have you experienced this past week as you have sought to fully live the Lord's standards?

Using the standards and teachings from *For the Strength of Youth*, write one goal to focus on this next week by each of the topics below.

GOAL

HOW I DRESS	
MY CONVERSATIONS	
MY BEHAVIOR	
LITERATURE I READ	
MOVIES I WATCH	
TELEVISION I WATCH	
HOW I USE THE INTERNET	
MUSIC I LISTEN TO	
HOW I USE MY CELL PHONE	
BEING SEXUALLY PURE	

TUESDAY NOVEMBER 29TH 2016	WEDNESDAY NOVEMBER 30TH 2016	THURSDAY DECEMBER 1ST 2016
☐ I HAD MORNING PRAYER ☐ I HAD EVENING PRAYER	☐ I HAD MORNING PRAYER ☐ I HAD EVENING PRAYER	☐ I HAD MORNING PRAYER ☐ I HAD EVENING PRAYER
☐ I STUDIED THE SCRIPTURES	☐ I STUDIED THE SCRIPTURES	☐ I STUDIED THE SCRIPTURES

SIGNIFICANT THINGS THAT HAPPENED TODAY

SPECIFIC THINGS I DID TODAY TO PRESS FORWARD FEASTING UPON THE WORD OF CHRIST

GOAL(S) FOR TOMORROW TO PRESS FORWARD FEASTING UPON THE WORD OF CHRIST

INTEGRITY: WHAT I DID TODAY TO LIVE UP TO THE LORD'S STANDARDS

December 2-4

FRIDAY **DECEMBER 2ND** 2016	SATURDAY **DECEMBER 3RD** 2016	SUNDAY **DECEMBER 4TH** 2016
☐ I HAD MORNING PRAYER ☐ I HAD EVENING PRAYER	☐ I HAD MORNING PRAYER ☐ I HAD EVENING PRAYER	☐ I HAD MORNING PRAYER ☐ I HAD EVENING PRAYER
☐ I STUDIED THE SCRIPTURES	☐ I STUDIED THE SCRIPTURES	☐ I STUDIED THE SCRIPTURES

SIGNIFICANT THINGS THAT HAPPENED TODAY

SPECIFIC THINGS I DID TODAY TO PRESS FORWARD ENDURING TO THE END

GOAL(S) FOR TOMORROW TO PRESS FORWARD ENDURING TO THE END

INTEGRITY: WHAT I DID TODAY TO LIVE UP TO THE LORD'S STANDARDS

The Sabbath Day

DECEMBER 4TH

 SACRAMENT MEETING WHAT ARE SOME SPECIFIC LESSONS YOU LEARNED & IMPRESSIONS YOU HAD DURING SACRAMENT MEETING?

CLASSES

WHAT IMPORTANT DOCTRINES & PRINCIPLES DID YOU LEARN IN YOUR CLASSES?

WHAT IS INTEGRITY?

What experiences, challenges, and blessings have you experienced this past week as you have sought to fully live the Lord's standards?

Using the standards and teachings from *For the Strength of Youth*, write one goal to focus on this next week by each of the topics below.

	GOAL
HOW I DRESS	
MY CONVERSATIONS	
MY BEHAVIOR	
LITERATURE I READ	
MOVIES I WATCH	
TELEVISION I WATCH	
HOW I USE THE INTERNET	
MUSIC I LISTEN TO	
HOW I USE MY CELL PHONE	
BEING SEXUALLY PURE	

December 5-7

PRESS FORWARD ENDURING TO THE END

	MONDAY **DECEMBER 5TH 2016**	TUESDAY **DECEMBER 6TH 2016**	WEDNESDAY **DECEMBER 7TH 2016**
	☐ I HAD MORNING PRAYER ☐ I HAD EVENING PRAYER	☐ I HAD MORNING PRAYER ☐ I HAD EVENING PRAYER	☐ I HAD MORNING PRAYER ☐ I HAD EVENING PRAYER
	☐ I STUDIED THE SCRIPTURES	☐ I STUDIED THE SCRIPTURES	☐ I STUDIED THE SCRIPTURES
SIGNIFICANT THINGS THAT HAPPENED TODAY			
SPECIFIC THINGS I DID TODAY TO PRESS FORWARD ENDURING TO THE END			
GOAL(S) FOR TOMORROW TO PRESS FORWARD ENDURING TO THE END			
INTEGRITY: WHAT I DID TODAY TO LIVE UP TO THE LORD'S STANDARDS			

THURSDAY DECEMBER 8TH 2016	FRIDAY DECEMBER 9TH 2016	SATURDAY DECEMBER 10TH 2016
☐ I HAD MORNING PRAYER ☐ I HAD EVENING PRAYER	☐ I HAD MORNING PRAYER ☐ I HAD EVENING PRAYER	☐ I HAD MORNING PRAYER ☐ I HAD EVENING PRAYER
☐ I STUDIED THE SCRIPTURES	☐ I STUDIED THE SCRIPTURES	☐ I STUDIED THE SCRIPTURES

SIGNIFICANT THINGS THAT HAPPENED TODAY

SPECIFIC THINGS I DID TODAY TO PRESS FORWARD ENDURING TO THE END

GOAL(S) FOR TOMORROW TO PRESS FORWARD ENDURING TO THE END

INTEGRITY: WHAT I DID TODAY TO LIVE UP TO THE LORD'S STANDARDS

The Sabbath Day
DECEMBER 11TH

 SACRAMENT MEETING WHAT ARE SOME SPECIFIC LESSONS YOU LEARNED & IMPRESSIONS YOU HAD DURING SACRAMENT MEETING?

 CLASSES WHAT IMPORTANT DOCTRINES & PRINCIPLES DID YOU LEARN IN YOUR CLASSES?

Personal Progress

INTEGRITY EXPERIENCE #1
(ONE MONTH CHALLENGE - WEEK 4)

WHAT IS INTEGRITY?

What experiences, challenges, and blessings have you experienced this past week as you have sought to fully live the Lord's standards?

Using the standards and teachings from *For the Strength of Youth*, write one goal to focus on this next week by each of the topics below.

	GOAL
HOW I DRESS	
MY CONVERSATIONS	
MY BEHAVIOR	
LITERATURE I READ	
MOVIES I WATCH	
TELEVISION I WATCH	
HOW I USE THE INTERNET	
MUSIC I LISTEN TO	
HOW I USE MY CELL PHONE	
BEING SEXUALLY PURE	

December 11-13

	SUNDAY DECEMBER 11TH 2016	MONDAY DECEMBER 12TH 2016	TUESDAY DECEMBER 13TH 2016
	☐ I HAD MORNING PRAYER ☐ I HAD EVENING PRAYER	☐ I HAD MORNING PRAYER ☐ I HAD EVENING PRAYER	☐ I HAD MORNING PRAYER ☐ I HAD EVENING PRAYER
	☐ I STUDIED THE SCRIPTURES	☐ I STUDIED THE SCRIPTURES	☐ I STUDIED THE SCRIPTURES
SIGNIFICANT THINGS THAT HAPPENED TODAY			
SPECIFIC THINGS I DID TODAY TO PRESS FORWARD ENDURING TO THE END			
GOAL(S) FOR TOMORROW TO PRESS FORWARD ENDURING TO THE END			
INTEGRITY: WHAT I DID TODAY TO LIVE UP TO THE LORD'S STANDARDS			

 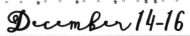

December 14-16

WEDNESDAY **DECEMBER 14**TH 2016	THURSDAY **DECEMBER 15**TH 2016	FRIDAY **DECEMBER 16**TH 2016
☐ I HAD MORNING PRAYER ☐ I HAD EVENING PRAYER	☐ I HAD MORNING PRAYER ☐ I HAD EVENING PRAYER	☐ I HAD MORNING PRAYER ☐ I HAD EVENING PRAYER
☐ I STUDIED THE SCRIPTURES	☐ I STUDIED THE SCRIPTURES	☐ I STUDIED THE SCRIPTURES

SIGNIFICANT THINGS THAT HAPPENED TODAY

SPECIFIC THINGS I DID TODAY TO PRESS FORWARD ENDURING TO THE END

GOAL(S) FOR TOMORROW TO PRESS FORWARD ENDURING TO THE END

INTEGRITY: WHAT I DID TODAY TO LIVE UP TO THE LORD'S STANDARDS

December 17-19

PRESS FORWARD ENDURING
TO THE END

	SATURDAY DECEMBER 17TH 2016	SUNDAY DECEMBER 18TH 2016	MONDAY DECEMBER 19TH 2016
	☐ I HAD MORNING PRAYER ☐ I HAD EVENING PRAYER	☐ I HAD MORNING PRAYER ☐ I HAD EVENING PRAYER	☐ I HAD MORNING PRAYER ☐ I HAD EVENING PRAYER
	☐ I STUDIED THE SCRIPTURES	☐ I STUDIED THE SCRIPTURES	☐ I STUDIED THE SCRIPTURES
SIGNIFICANT THINGS THAT HAPPENED TODAY			
SPECIFIC THINGS I DID TODAY TO PRESS FORWARD ENDURING TO THE END			
GOAL(S) FOR TOMORROW TO PRESS FORWARD ENDURING TO THE END			
INTEGRITY: WHAT I DID TODAY TO LIVE UP TO THE LORD'S STANDARDS			

SACRAMENT MEETING

WHAT ARE SOME SPECIFIC LESSONS YOU LEARNED & IMPRESSIONS YOU HAD DURING SACRAMENT MEETING?

CLASSES

WHAT IMPORTANT DOCTRINES & PRINCIPLES DID YOU LEARN IN YOUR CLASSES?

Personal Progress
INTEGRITY EXPERIENCE #2

MY INTEGRITY

Conduct a self-assessment of your personal integrity. Reflect upon the following questions and record your answers below:

DO I AVOID GOSSIP?

DO I AVOID INAPPROPRIATE JOKES?

DO I AVOID SWEARING & PROFANITY?

DO I AVOID BEING LIGHT-MINDED ABOUT SACRED SUBJECTS?

AM I COMPLETELY TRUTHFUL?

AM I MORALLY CLEAN?

AM I HONEST?

AM I DEPENDABLE?

AM I TRUSTWORTHY IN MY SCHOOLWORK?

AM I TRUSTWORTHY IN ALL MY ACTIVITIES?

Challenge: Pray daily for strength and for the guidance of the Holy Ghost to help you live with integrity. Write in your journal the things you can do to improve your personal integrity and at least one new habit you want to develop.

 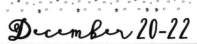

December 20-22

TUESDAY DECEMBER 20TH 2016	WEDNESDAY DECEMBER 21ST 2016	THURSDAY DECEMBER 22ND 2016
☐ I HAD MORNING PRAYER	☐ I HAD MORNING PRAYER	☐ I HAD MORNING PRAYER
☐ I HAD EVENING PRAYER	☐ I HAD EVENING PRAYER	☐ I HAD EVENING PRAYER
☐ I STUDIED THE SCRIPTURES	☐ I STUDIED THE SCRIPTURES	☐ I STUDIED THE SCRIPTURES
☐ I PRAYED FOR STRENGTH TO LIVE WITH INTEGRITY	☐ I PRAYED FOR STRENGTH TO LIVE WITH INTEGRITY	☐ I PRAYED FOR STRENGTH TO LIVE WITH INTEGRITY

SIGNIFICANT THINGS THAT HAPPENED TODAY

SPECIFIC THINGS I DID TODAY TO PRESS FORWARD ENDURING TO THE END

GOAL(S) FOR TOMORROW TO PRESS FORWARD ENDURING TO THE END

WHAT I DID TODAY TO LIVE WITH INTEGRITY

December 23-25

PRESS FORWARD ENDURING
TO THE END

	FRIDAY **DECEMBER 23RD** 2016	SATURDAY **DECEMBER 24TH** 2016	SUNDAY **DECEMBER 25TH** 2016
	☐ I HAD MORNING PRAYER	☐ I HAD MORNING PRAYER	☐ I HAD MORNING PRAYER
	☐ I HAD EVENING PRAYER	☐ I HAD EVENING PRAYER	☐ I HAD EVENING PRAYER
	☐ I STUDIED THE SCRIPTURES	☐ I STUDIED THE SCRIPTURES	☐ I STUDIED THE SCRIPTURES
	☐ I PRAYED FOR STRENGTH TO LIVE WITH INTEGRITY	☐ I PRAYED FOR STRENGTH TO LIVE WITH INTEGRITY	☐ I PRAYED FOR STRENGTH TO LIVE WITH INTEGRITY
SIGNIFICANT THINGS THAT HAPPENED TODAY			
SPECIFIC THINGS I DID TODAY TO PRESS FORWARD ENDURING TO THE END			
GOAL(S) FOR TOMORROW TO PRESS FORWARD ENDURING TO THE END			
WHAT I DID TODAY TO LIVE WITH INTEGRITY			

SACRAMENT MEETING

WHAT ARE SOME SPECIFIC LESSONS YOU LEARNED & IMPRESSIONS YOU HAD DURING SACRAMENT MEETING?

CLASSES

WHAT IMPORTANT DOCTRINES & PRINCIPLES DID YOU LEARN IN YOUR CLASSES?

INTEGRITY EXPERIENCE #3

THE SAVIOR: AN EXAMPLE OF INTEGRITY

The Savior is the perfect example of integrity; He did what He promised the Father He would do. The scriptures are full of other people who lived with integrity. Read the following scriptures, and in each box, record what each person did as an example of living with integrity.

Jesus Christ 3 NEPHI 11:10–11	*Joseph of Egypt* GENESIS 39
Esther BOOK OF ESTHER	*Job* JOB 2:3; 27:3–6
Shadrach, Meshach, & Abed-nego DANIEL 3 AND 6	*Paul* ACTS 26
Hyrum Smith D&C 124:15	*Joseph Smith* JOSEPH SMITH—HISTORY 1:21–25

COURAGE TO SHOW INTEGRITY

Think of a time when you had the courage to show integrity, especially when it was not easy or popular. Write about it below.

December 26-28

MONDAY **DECEMBER 26**TH 2016	TUESDAY **DECEMBER 27**TH 2016	WEDNESDAY **DECEMBER 28**TH 2016
☐ I HAD MORNING PRAYER	☐ I HAD MORNING PRAYER	☐ I HAD MORNING PRAYER
☐ I HAD EVENING PRAYER	☐ I HAD EVENING PRAYER	☐ I HAD EVENING PRAYER
☐ I STUDIED THE SCRIPTURES	☐ I STUDIED THE SCRIPTURES	☐ I STUDIED THE SCRIPTURES
☐ I PRAYED FOR STRENGTH TO LIVE WITH INTEGRITY	☐ I PRAYED FOR STRENGTH TO LIVE WITH INTEGRITY	☐ I PRAYED FOR STRENGTH TO LIVE WITH INTEGRITY

SIGNIFICANT THINGS THAT HAPPENED TODAY

SPECIFIC THINGS I DID TODAY TO PRESS FORWARD ENDURING TO THE END

GOAL(S) FOR TOMORROW TO PRESS FORWARD ENDURING TO THE END

WHAT I DID TODAY TO LIVE WITH INTEGRITY

December 29-31

PRESS FORWARD ENDURING TO THE END

THURSDAY **DECEMBER 29TH** 2016	FRIDAY **DECEMBER 30TH** 2016	SATURDAY **DECEMBER 31ST** 2016
□ I HAD MORNING PRAYER □ I HAD EVENING PRAYER	□ I HAD MORNING PRAYER □ I HAD EVENING PRAYER	□ I HAD MORNING PRAYER □ I HAD EVENING PRAYER
□ I STUDIED THE SCRIPTURES	□ I STUDIED THE SCRIPTURES	□ I STUDIED THE SCRIPTURES
□ I PRAYED FOR STRENGTH TO LIVE WITH INTEGRITY	□ I PRAYED FOR STRENGTH TO LIVE WITH INTEGRITY	□ I PRAYED FOR STRENGTH TO LIVE WITH INTEGRITY

SIGNIFICANT THINGS THAT HAPPENED TODAY

SPECIFIC THINGS I DID TODAY TO PRESS FORWARD ENDURING TO THE END

GOAL(S) FOR TOMORROW TO PRESS FORWARD ENDURING TO THE END

WHAT I DID TODAY TO LIVE WITH INTEGRITY

WHEREFORE, YE MUST

Press Forward

WITH A STEADFASTNESS IN CHRIST, HAVING A PERFECT BRIGHTNESS OF HOPE, AND A LOVE OF GOD
AND OF ALL MEN. WHEREFORE, IF YE SHALL PRESS FORWARD, FEASTING UPON THE WORD OF CHRIST,
AND ENDURE TO THE END, BEHOLD, THUS SAITH THE FATHER: YE SHALL HAVE ETERNAL LIFE.

2 Nephi 31:20

HOW DID THIS SCRIPTURE MAKE A DIFFERENCE IN YOUR LIFE THIS YEAR?

Personal Progress

FIRST ADDITIONAL INTEGRITY EXPERIENCE

YOU MUST FULFILL 3 ADDITIONAL "INTEGRITY" EXPERIENCES.
USE THIS PAGE TO COMPLETE ONE OF THE ADDITIONAL EXPERIENCES
FOUND IN YOUR PERSONAL PROGRESS BOOK.

Personal Progress
SECOND ADDITIONAL INTEGRITY EXPERIENCE

Personal Progress

YOU MUST FULFILL 3 ADDITIONAL "INTEGRITY" EXPERIENCES. USE THIS PAGE TO COMPLETE ONE OF THE ADDITIONAL EXPERIENCES FOUND IN YOUR PERSONAL PROGRESS BOOK.

WHAT IS VIRTUE?

- Virtue is a pattern of thought and behavior based on high moral standards.
- It includes chastity and purity.
- The power to create mortal life is an exalted power God has given His children.
- He has commanded that this power be used only between a man and a woman, lawfully wedded as husband and wife.

Study the meaning and importance of chastity and virtue by reading the references below. By each reference write or doodle what you learn about the teachings and promised blessings of being sexually pure.

MORONI 9:9

JACOB 2:28

ARTICLE OF FAITH #13

"SEXUAL PURITY" IN FOR THE STRENGTH OF YOUTH

THE FAMILY: A PROCLAMATION TO THE WORLD

PROVERBS 31:10-31

My Commitment Write about your own commitment to be chaste.

Personal Progress

VIRTUE & THE HOLY GHOST

Draw or doodle a picture that depicts the teachings in the following phrases.

Virtuous living "at all times and in all things, and in all places" qualifies you for the constant companionship of the Holy Ghost.

When you are baptized and confirmed, you are given the gift of the Holy Ghost to guide all aspects of your life.

Since the Holy Ghost does not dwell in unclean tabernacles, living a virtuous life is a prerequisite to having the companionship of the Holy Ghost and receiving the blessings of temple ordinances.

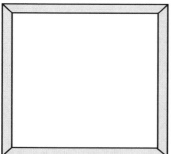
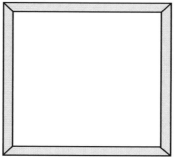
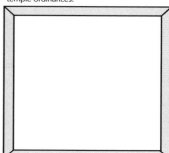

In each circle doodle or write the promised blessings in each scripture.

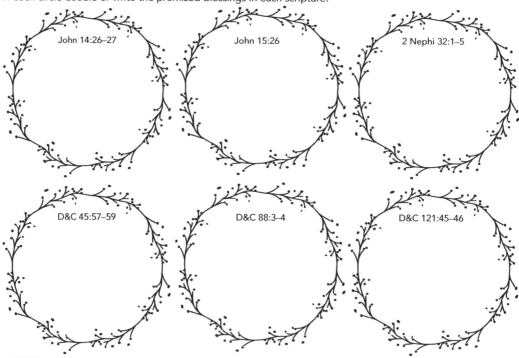

John 14:26–27

John 15:26

2 Nephi 32:1–5

D&C 45:57–59

D&C 88:3–4

D&C 121:45–46

Write about a time when you felt the guidance of the Holy Ghost.

Study Alma 5 in your scriptures. Mark all of the questions Alma asks. Count them and write the number of questions he asks in the box:

Choose 7 of the questions Alma asks and answer them for yourself. Write the question in the left column and the answer in the right column.

Make a list of the things you can and will do to prepare yourself to be pure and worthy to enter the temple and receive all the blessings our Heavenly Father has promised His beloved daughters.

240

Personal Progress

WE CAN REPENT

Because the Savior loves you and has given His life for you, you can repent. Repentance is an act of faith in Jesus Christ. Study the following references and doodle, draw, or write what they teach you about repentance.

MORONI 10:32–33

BOOK OF ENOS

"REPENTANCE"
FOR THE STRENGTH OF YOUTH

Read the sacrament prayers in Doctrine and Covenants 20:77, 79. Determine to partake worthily of the sacrament each week and fill your life with virtuous activities that will bring spiritual power. As you do this, you will grow stronger in your ability to resist temptation, keep the commandments, and become more like Jesus Christ. Determine what you can do daily to remain pure and worthy. Make a plan below.

My Plan:

49605863R00135